环球雅思连锁学校指定教材　全国雅思学
中国雅思标准教程　○基础培训

雅思写作

基础标准教程

IELTS Writing

团结出版社

图书在版编目（CIP）数据

环球雅思基础课程全国统一专用教材：基础全项课程：雅思写作基础标准教程/
环球雅思教材研究中心GTRC编写.—北京：团结出版社，2008.10
ISBN 978-7-80214-509-2

Ⅰ.环… Ⅱ.基… Ⅲ.英语-写作-高等教育-教材 Ⅳ.H315

中国版本图书馆CIP数据核字（2008）第166368号

出 版：团结出版社
（北京市东城区东皇城根南街84号 邮编：100006）
电 话：（010）65228880 65244790（总编室）
（010）62127297（发行）
网 址：http://www.tjpress.com
E-mail：65244790@163.com
经 销：全国新华书店
印 刷：北京市大兴区兴达印刷厂

开 本：185×260毫米
印 张：9
字 数：60千字
印 数：10000
印 次：2010年6月第3次印刷

书 号：978-7-80214-509-2/H•37
定 价：200.00 元（全套共4册）

坚持改变人生（代序）

从1997年环球雅思第1个学生开始，到今天拥有全国65所学校一年近25万学生，环球雅思已开创了中国培训界的领先品牌。我想这本书会影响数百万新时代年轻人的未来人生，也许就像这次雅思学习历程一样，充满坚毅、勇气、有志、有恒、有为……学习雅思，走向世界，成就自己人生辉煌的一刻。

我在创建环球雅思的这几年中，一直抱着对一件事情始终充满热情的心态，其中虽饱尝艰辛、历经无数当初看来无法逾越的困难，但我始终坚持下来了，从没有把眼前雅思的成功当成美好愿望的实现。

1997年12月的冬天，我独自一人，用订书机装订的10本18页复印纸的“最新”雅思备考教材在使馆门前兜售时，开始了我的环球雅思教育人生之旅，当时没有蓝图、没有方向，只有对教育的热忱、对雅思的执着，10年后，环球雅思品牌终于被芸芸学子喜爱认可。

每一个打开这本书，来到环球雅思追求理想人生的学生，都是有梦想、有追求的，坚持就有你成功的希望。

毅力不是每分每秒的“艰苦忍耐”，真正的毅力是清楚自己的人生目标，愿意承担这份责任和辛苦，有颗坚强又充满着希望的心。

善于学习的人能领会和掌握未来，好学的人懂得把观察、经验和知识转化为智慧并使用得当，不仅能持之以恒，更懂得如何事半功倍。

各位学子，你们的人生也许会在“学习雅思、走向海外”的这一刻而改变，全力以赴，让我们和优秀的老师们一起为你们的灿烂人生添砖加瓦，加油起航吧！

环球雅思学校总校长

环球天下教育科技集团总裁

张永琪

雅思考试的秘诀——善假于物也

荀子在《劝学》中说道："假舆马者，非利足也，而致千里；假舟楫者，非能水也，而绝江河。君子性非异也，善假于物也。"可见，善假于物是成功的捷径。在当今信息极其丰富的时代，"善假于物"又有更高的涵义，那就是一定要"假于"最专业、最老到的独门利器。

对于立志通过雅思考试的莘莘学子们而言，本套教材无疑是你可信赖的独门利器！那么，为什么本套教材称得上是独门利器呢？答案在于它们的作者——环球雅思全国的资深教师们！作为环球雅思连锁学校英语教学的精英，环球雅思学校的老师们正以自己的努力树立起雅思培训的卓越标杆。这些环雅的资深教师，在十年时间里见证过了数以万计的中国雅思考生通过雅思考试。每一本雅思图书，都倾注了环球雅思全体老师的全部心血，融入了他们近十年的教学经验。这些心血和经验，在我们图书的字里行间都得到完美体现！

另外，在这里特别感谢我们环球雅思的总校长张永琪先生，正是我们这样一名英明的校长，这样一位伯乐，不断引进优秀教师，使我们的雅思图书事业蓬勃发展。这套雅思教材系列丛书的出版正是环球雅思学校送给广大考生的一份厚礼。

在本套图书付梓出版之际，特别感谢以下提及的环球雅思全国学校各位老师在听、说、读、写、词汇、语法各科教材中的主持编写工作：卢峭梅、王陆、余波、杨凡、吴艳、李一萌、于光、王燕、李宁、江涛、孙维娟、刘丹妮、陈婷婷、张强、赵雪、高洁、曾丽娟、王辉、西震、李婷婷、王建军、齐辙、刘家玮、杨涛、杨童、何蓉、李超、赵婷、鲁成英、白杨、齐辙、闫冰、张志华、赵燕、王洪川、王丽萍、邹卓、杨飞、秦平、李向、贾丽娟、徐子群，同时感谢全体环雅老师。

谨以此套教材丛书献给大家，"君子性非异也，善假于物也。"

北京环球卓尔英才文化传播有限公司

教材组

2010 年 6 月

CONTENTS

目录

第一章 雅思写作综合介绍

IELTS写作部分测试要求学生在60分钟内完成两篇文章的写作。写作考试分为学术类（Academic）和移民类（General training）两种，单项满分为9分。

学术类（Academic）写作TASK 1 要求考生对图表（包括曲线图、柱状图、饼状图、流程图和表格）进行描述、解释和说明，字数不少于150个单词。

学术类（Academic）写作TASK 2 要求考生写一篇情景议论文，字数不少于250个单词。

移民类（General training）写作TASK 1 要求考生写一封英文信，为考生设定一个场景，要求考生写信咨询、投诉、感谢、邀请、道歉、给出建议或提出申请等，字数不少于150个单词。

移民类（General training）写作TASK 2 要求考生写一篇情景议论文，字数不少于250个单词。

学术类（Academic）写作和移民类（General training）写作TASK 1 难度不同，学术类（Academic）写作要求更高，而且图表写作也是中国考生平时练习较少，不好掌握的部分，相比较而言，移民类（General training）写作难度稍低。两类考试TASK 2 的难度相当，题目类型和话题背景类似。

第二章　英文写作基础知识

I 英语句子的成分

1. 主语

1) Old people should offer young people opportunities to practice their abilities and talents.
2) We should not overestimate or deny either of them.
3) Smoking is just a personal hobby and for entertainment.
4) It is hard to come to an absolute conclusion.
5) It is obvious that wearing uniforms would make school life dull and monotonous.

2. 谓语

1) They insist that the practice of censorship should be abolished.
2) Children should achieve success through their own efforts.
3) Advertising adds to the cost of goods.
4) In other aspects, computer affects people's daily life and does harm to people.
5) Nowadays, more and more people agree that smoking is an unwholesome hobby, which is equivalent to suicide.

3. 表语

1) Censorship is a violation of people's freedom of expression.
2) The methods of farming and slaughter of these animals are often barbaric and cruel.
3) Love is time-consuming and tears students away from learning, the students' main task.
4) What we should do is to tell children how to solve these problems properly.
5) What they emphasize is that formal examinations are harmful to students' creativity.

4. 宾语

1) Junk food impairs people's health.
2) You've even started bringing work home and you keep working until the wee hours of the morning.
3) Studies reveal that there is a definite link between smoking and some serious diseases such as lung cancer and heart disease.
4) It brings us a lot of pleasure and amusement.

5. 定语

1) It is hard to come to an absolute conclusion.
2) In recent years, the Internet has been gaining popularity at an amazing rate.
3) Individuals with limited budgets usually get their priorities right.
4) Those people who strongly oppose the practice claim that it violates people's basic rights of working.

6. 状语

1) Outdoor activities can improve our health greatly.
2) According to the laws, advertisements must be completely truthful and healthy.
3) To dispel loneliness and kill the time, they can cultivate some other hobbies such as growing flowers, collecting stamps and learning to paint.
4) Living far away from home, one will suffer from loneliness and homesickness.
5) I still like to travel with friends because I think the most important thing during travel is to get pleasure and relaxation.

7. 同位语

1) Shopping, a necessary activity in everyday life is more convenient in the city.
2) Love can tear students away from learning, the students' main task.
3) But the disadvantage of this solution lies in the fact that too much land that could be used for farming or housing will inevitably be occupied by more and more roads.

8. 补语

1) We consider compulsory military service a violation of human rights.
2) Cloning technology can make humans redundant, replaceable and even extinct.
3) I find the employment situation frustrating.

II 英语句子的基本结构

英语句子的结构虽然较为复杂，却有章可循，掌握了这些常用结构对提高阅读和写作能力都有很大的帮助。归纳起来，英语主要有以下几种基本句型：

1. S+V (主语+动词—不及物)

1) Views on the issue in question vary from person to person.
2) The Era of Globalization has already come.

2. S+V+O(主语+动词/及物动词+宾语)

1) They are discussing the benefits and risks of smoking.
2) The chemical waste endangers people's health.
3) The advocates render the reasons for their position.

注意：不及物动词可以通过跟介词或副词结合构成及物动词。

1) Vi.+Pre = Vt. deal with, look into, complain about, laugh at, look after
2) Vi.+Adv+Pre = Vt. make up for, look down upon, end up in
3) Vi.+N+Pre = Vt. take care of, take advantage of, make use of, put an end to, attach greater importance to, lay emphasis on

3. S+V+O2+O1 (主语+动词+间接宾语/人+直接宾语/物)

1) Learning foreign languages just offers us such a good approach.
2) We can show them that earning money is not easy, and they should spend the money carefully.
3) Raising pets gives them great happiness and helps relieve their pressure and depression.

4. S+V+O+OC (主语+动词+宾语+宾语补足语)

1) We consider the practice of censorship a violation of human rights.
2) We never found it difficult to occupy our spare time.
3) Every scene on the screen keeps me up-to-date.
4) Art funding may make artists shift the focus from creativity to pleasing funding bodies.

5. S+LV+SC（主语+系动词+表语）

be, seem, appear, look, remain, sound, feel, smell, taste, become, grow, turn, go prove, etc.

1) Overpopulation could become a serious worldwide threat.
2) Environmental protection and the protection of biodiversity are a luxury for developing nations.
3) They believe the violence they see is normal and acceptable.
4) Taking animals as the source of food and clothes appears much more practical.

III 英语句子的结构分类

1. 简单句

1) Television can widen our horizons.
2) Students can get opportunities to experience a totally different culture.
3) They enrich our cultural life.
4) It brings us a lot of pleasure and amusement.
5) More importantly, relatives, neighbors and his teachers should give the very kid as much love as possible to make him feel least abandoned.

2. 并列句

1) Solving the problem of traffic jams is not an easy job and I don't think any individual or organization can easily handle it.
2) Some people are indulged in raising pets and they would feel uncomfortable and lonely if they were forbidden to do so.
3) With the steady growth in the country's economy as well as the people's living standard, the rhythm of people's living is speeding up and a lot of changes have taken place in their daily life.
4) In the countryside, the air is clean, the food is fresh and the houses are usually spacious with large yards around them.
5) Some professors prefer to control discussion, while others prefer to guide the class without dominating it.
6) Television hasn't been with us all that long, but we are already beginning to forget what

the world was like without it.

7) I used to meet several vegetarians but I have never heard of a nation that advocates vegetarian diet.

3. 复合句

1) They insist that the practice of censorship should be abolished.
2) It is evident that it can relieve the traffic congestion in the streets, thus accelerating the flow of buses and cars.
3) At that moment only a language that can be accepted and understood by most of the people such as English, French, Arabian and so on will function.
4) However, we cannot think that parents should accept responsibility and be punished if their children behave badly.
5) But the problem is that the cost for telephone calls is so high that many cannot afford it.
6) Nowadays, more and more people agree that smoking is an unwholesome hobby, which is equivalent to committing suicide.

第三章 英语写作常用句型范例

I 定语从句

1. that which who引导的定语从句

1) The main reason that everyone can see is that television presents a vivid world in front of us.
每个人能都看到的主要原因是，电视在我们面前展现了一个生动形象的世界。

2) Another factor we must consider is that television plays an educational role in our daily lives.
我们必须考虑的另一个因素是电视在我们的日常生活中起到教育的作用。

3) Those people who strongly oppose the practice claim that it violates people's basic rights of working.
强烈反对这种做法的人声称它侵犯了人们基本的工作权利。

4) Those who welcome the internet hold that it brings us great convenience and efficiency.
赞成网络的人认为它给我们带来了很大的方便和效率。

5) There are many other factors that bring about the problem.
有很多其他因素导致这个问题。

6) There are still some people who hold that we should travel with friends.
还有一些人认为我们应该与朋友一起去旅行。

7) They believe the violence they see is normal and acceptable.
他们相信他们所看到的暴力是正常的和可接受的。

8) During a short vacation, the only thing I can do is stay at home, sleep, eat and make myself fatter and fatter.
在短假期里，我能做的惟一的事就是待在家里，又睡又吃，使自己越来越胖。

2. where when why whose引导的定语从句

1) We live in a country where people enjoy their legal rights.
我们生活在人们享有合法权利的国家。

2) There are numerous reasons why I hold this opinion.
我之所以持有这个观点是有很多原因的。

3. 介词前置的定语从句

1) I hit upon an article in which some people hold that students should wear uniforms every day.
我看到一篇文章，其中写道，一些人认为中学生应该每天都穿校服。

2) In kindergartens, there are many educational facilities from which children can benefit.
幼儿园有很多教育设施，孩子们可以从中受益。

3) The critics argue that the practice does not coincide with the present-day civilized world in which liberty and individuality are highly worshiped.
批评家们认为这种做法与目前高度尊崇自由和个性的文明社会不一致。

4. 非限制性定语从句

1) They want to imitate what they see, which is sometimes dangerous.
他们想要模仿他们所看到的东西，这在有时是危险的。

2) Mothers can concentrate on their work and advance their careers, which is also helpful to social development.
母亲们可以集中于她们的工作，发展她们的事业，这对社会发展也是有利的。

3) It is a controversial question, which has aroused heated discussion among people.
这是一个有争议的问题，它引起了人们的热烈讨论。

4) Nowadays, more and more people agree that smoking is an unwholesome hobby, one that is equivalent to committing suicide.
现在，越来越多的人同意吸烟是一个不健康的爱好，它等同于自杀。

5) The elderly can look after their grandchildren, which may, to some degree, relieve the pressure from the younger generation.
老年人可以照看他们的孙辈，这也会在一定程度上减轻年轻人的压力。

6) Some students spend too much time playing computer games, which is harmful to their health and has a negative influence on their studies.
一些学生在玩计算机游戏上花费了太多的时间，这对他们的身体有害，也会影响他们的学习。

II 状语从句

1. 原因状语从句

1) I still like to travel with friends because I think the most important thing during a trip is to get pleasure and relaxation.
我还是喜欢和朋友一起旅行，因为我认为在旅行中最重要的是得到快乐和休息。

2) I think it is sagacious to raise pets because it is beneficial in many ways.
我认为饲养宠物是明智的，因为这在很多方面都有好处。

3) Some people suggest that we shouldn't help the adventurers, because any kind of help would ruin their pleasure of exploring.
一些人认为我们不应该帮助探险者，因为任何形式的帮助都会破坏他们探险的乐趣。

2. 让步状语从句

1) Although it is indispensable to human beings, it has also brought a lot of inconvenience.
虽然它对人类必不可少，它也给我们带来了很多的不便。

2) While the small family has a unique advantage, it cannot compete with the large family.
虽然小家庭有独特的优点，但它在很多方面不能和大家庭竞争。

3) Most people marry and have children, so they need a steady, reliable income because of their family responsibilities, even if they are dissatisfied with their jobs.
大多数的人结婚并且有孩子，所以他们为了他们的家庭责任需要稳定的可靠的收入，即使他们不满意他们的工作。

4) Some people suggest that we should not help the adventurers even if they are in danger, because any kind of help would ruin their pleasure of exploring.
一些人认为我们不应该帮助探险者，即使他们处于危险中，因为任何形式的帮助都会破坏他们探险的乐趣。

5) Reasonable and attractive as the opinion seems, it does not hold water.
这个观点虽然看起来有道理和吸引人，但是它经不起推敲。

6) Nowadays, people face fierce competition and suffer greatly from life's pressures, so they spend little time with their families, even though they want to.
现在，人们面临激烈的竞争，承受巨大的压力，所以几乎没有时间和家人在一起，虽然他们想这么做。

3. 条件状语从句

1) If smoking is totally banned, more serious problems such as unemployment will arise.
如果吸烟被全面禁止，更严重的问题就会产生，如失业。

2) If you leave your present job, you'll have to start at a much lower position.
如果你离开你现在的工作，你不得不从一个低得多的职位上重新开始。

3) If we tear down the old buildings, we are ruining the cultural heritage, the traditional value as well.
如果我们推倒老建筑，我们就破坏了文化遗产和传统价值。

4) If they continue to work in a way their health permits, old people can still make a great contribution to the society.
如果他们继续以他们的健康允许的方式工作，老年人仍然会为社会做很大的贡献。

（四）时间状语从句

1) When one finishes his study abroad, he or she will have more opportunities for his or her future career.
当一个人完成留学时，他将会有更多的机会开拓未来的事业。

2) Telephones are very convenient, especially when we have an urgent situation.
电话是非常方便的，尤其当我们有紧急的事情时。

III 并列句

1) Solving the problem of traffic jams is not an easy job and I don't think any individual or organization can easily handle it.
解决交通拥挤问题不是一个容易的工作，我不认为任何个人或单位能很容易地解决它。

2) Some people are indulged in raising pets and they would feel uncomfortable and lonely if they were forbidden to do so.
一些人沉溺于饲养宠物，如果他们被禁止饲养宠物，他们会感到不舒服和孤独。

3) With the steady growth in the country's economy as well as the people's living standard, the rhythm of people's living is speeding up and a lot of changes have taken place in their daily life.
随着国家经济的增长和人民生活水平的提高，人们生活的节奏加快了，他们的日常生活发生了很多变化。

4) In the countryside, the air is clean, the food is fresh and the houses are usually spacious with large yards around them.
在乡村，空气是干净的，食物是新鲜的，房子通常是宽敞的，四周环绕宽大的庭院。

IV 并列谓语

1) Raising pets gives them great happiness and helps relieve their stress.
饲养宠物给他们带来很大的快乐而且帮助他们减轻缓解压力。

2) Nowadays, young people face fierce competition and suffer from great life pressure.
现在年轻人面临激烈的竞争，承受很大的生活压力。

3) Wearing uniforms, to some extent, discourages individuality and hinders the development of creativity.
在某种程度上，穿校服不鼓励个性，阻碍创造力的发展。

4) They bring great pleasures to young people, train them to respond quickly and arouse their interest in computer science.
他们给年轻人带来很大的快乐，训练他们反应迅速，激起他们对计算机科学的兴趣。

V 动名词短语

1) Smoking is just a personal hobby and entertainment.
吸烟只是一种个人爱好和娱乐。

2) Playing games does not require students to use any of their creativity.
玩游戏不要求学生们使用任何的创造力。

3) Nowadays raising pets such as dogs and cats in big cities is becoming more and more popular.
现在，饲养宠物如猫和狗在大城市里正在变得越来越流行。

4) Many students are not used to taking care of themselves.
很多学生不习惯于自己照顾自己。

5) Family plays an important role in shaping children's characters.
家庭在塑造孩子的性格方面起到重要的作用。

6) Living on campus is beneficial to the students not only academically but also

psychologically.

住在校园里对学生有益处，不仅在学术上，而且在心理上。

VI 宾语从句

1) They want to imitate what they see.
   他们想要模仿他们所看到的东西。
2) From friends, we can learn what we need.
   从朋友那里，我们能学到我们需要的东西。
3) Studies reveal that there is a definite link between smoking and some serious diseases such as lung cancer and heart disease.
   研究表明，在吸烟和一些严重的疾病如肺癌和心脏病之间，有确定的联系。
4) They insist that the practice of censorship should be abolished.
   他们认为审查的做法应该被废除。
5) Some think that the school should be more responsible for children's education compared with the parents.
   一些人认为，与父母相比，学校更应负责孩子的教育。
6) We need to know where we can buy these products.
   我们需要知道在哪里能买到这些产品。
7) Some people suggest that the old people's children have the obligation to look after their old parents.
   一些人认为，子女有义务照看他们的父母。

VII 主语从句

1) What the old need is spiritual consolation.
   老年人需要的是精神安慰。
2) What we should do is to tell children how to solve these problems properly.
   我们应该做的是，告诉孩子们如何正确地解决这些问题。
3) It is obvious that wearing the uniforms would make school life dull and monotonous.
   穿校服会使学校生活乏味单调，这是显然的。

4) It is well known that there is a clear link between smoking and some kinds of serious diseases.
众所周知，吸烟和一些严重的疾病之间有清楚的联系。

5) It is sagacious that all relevant factors should be taken into account before taking any action.
在采取任何行动前，所有相关的因素都应该被考虑，这是明智的。

6) Whether young people should study abroad should be left to individuals to judge.
年轻人是否应该出国留学，这应该留给个人去判断。

7) Whether students should wear uniforms is a controversial issue.
中学生是不是应该穿校服，这是一个有争议的问题。

VIII 表语从句

1) What they emphasize is that formal examinations are harmful to students' creativity.
他们强调的是考试对学生的创造力有害。

2) The first reason is that raising pets is harmful to people's health.
第一个原因是饲养宠物对人的健康有害。

IX 分词短语

1) Living far away from home, one will suffer from loneliness and homesickness.
远离家庭生活，人要忍受孤独和思乡。

2) They spend too much time in front of the television, ignoring their studies, outdoor activities and even their family.
他们在电视前花费了太多的时间，忽略了他们的学习、户外活动，甚至他们的家庭。

3) Compared with a large family, a small family has a unique advantage.
和大家庭相比，小家庭有一个独特的优点。

4) Nowadays, there are more and more young people going to study abroad.
现在出国留学的年轻人越来越多。

5) You can always see young people and even adults addicted to computer games.
你总能看到沉溺于计算机游戏中的年轻人，甚至成年人。

6) There are some disadvantages brought about by raising pets.
有些弊端由饲养宠物引起。

7) Children are hurt by pets raised by their family.
孩子们被他们家饲养的宠物所伤害。

8) Smoking costs a large sum of money, laying a huge economic burden on the smoker's family.
吸烟花费大量的钱，给吸烟者的家庭带来巨大的经济负担。

9) The commodities and services provided by society have become more diversified.
由社会提供的商品和服务已经变得更多样化。

X 同位语和同位语从句

1) Shopping, a necessary activity in everyday life is more convenient in the city.
购物，这个每天生活中必需的活动，在城市里是更方便的。

2) Love can tear students away from learning, the students' main task.
爱情能将学生从学习，学生的主要工作中分开。

3) Some people even propose a suggestion that smoking should be totally banned in all public places.
一些人甚至提出了建议，在所有公共场所完全禁止吸烟。

4) From what I have mentioned above, it is not difficult to get the conclusion that students should go abroad to study.
从上面我所提到的，不难得出这样一个结论：中学生应该出国留学。

XI 平行结构

1) I stayed at home, sleeping, eating and making myself fatter and fatter.
我待在家里，又睡又吃，使自己越来越胖。

2) They spend too much time in front of the television, ignoring their studies, outdoor activities and even their family.
他们在电视前花费了太多的时间，忽略了他们的学习、户外活动，甚至他们的家庭。

3) To dispel loneliness and kill time, they can cultivate some other hobbies such as growing flowers, collecting stamps and learning to paint.

为了赶走孤独和消磨时光，他们可以培养其他的爱好，比如养花、集邮和学习绘画。

倒装

1) Only in this way, can the problem be solved successfully.
只有用这种方式，这个问题才能成功地解决。

2) Only if one has enough self-control, can he benefit from playing games.
只有当一个人有足够的自控能力时，他才能从玩游戏中获益。

3) From my teacher, not only do I learn the knowledge in books, but also I gain some spiritual development.
从老师那里，不仅我学到了书本上的知识，而且我获得了很多精神上的东西。

XIII 插入语

1) Many people, however, argue that children should be looked after in the kindergarten.
然而，很多人认为儿童应该在幼儿园被照看。

2) Solving problems in the dorm will, in the long run, help students understand how to communicate with others.
解决宿舍中的问题从长远看将帮助学生们懂得如何与其他人打交道。

XIV 不定式短语

1) It is hard to come to an absolute conclusion.
要得到一个绝对的结论是困难的。

2) It is inevitable for the old to have a generation gap with their children.
对老年人来说，和他们的孩子们有代沟是不可避免的。

3) The practice of censorship helps maintain a stable and orderly society.
审查的做法有助于维持一个稳定和有秩序的社会。

4) What we should do is tell the children how to solve these problems properly.
我们应该做的是告诉孩子们如何正确地解决这些问题。

5) To dispel loneliness and kill time, they can cultivate some other hobbies such as growing flowers, collecting stamps and learning to paint.
为了赶走孤独和消磨时光，他们可以培养其他的爱好，比如养花、集邮和学习绘画。

6) It brings us serious problems to solve.
它给我们带来了需要解决的严重的问题。

XV 介词短语

1) According to the laws, advertisements must be completely truthful and healthy.
根据法律，广告必须是完全真实的和健康的。

2) Thanks to the development of medical science, people live longer than before.
因为医学的发展，人们的寿命比过去长。

3) With the limited budget, the government is unable to invest much money in education.
预算很有限，政府不能投资很多钱在教育上。

4) With the development of society and the improvement of people's living standard, a lot of changes have taken place in their daily life.
随着社会的发展和人民生活水平的提高，他们的日常生活发生了很多变化。

5) Without formal examinations, it will be hard for universities to select qualified candidates.
若没有考试，大学很难选择合适的候选人。

XVI 被动句

1) Important events are often broadcast on live television.
电视上经常直播重要的事件。

2) On the contrary, some people are attracted to the convenience of the city.
相反，一些人被城市的便利所吸引。

3) When a person reaches his old age, he is forced to retire from his position. 当一个人到老年的时候，他被迫从他的岗位上退休。

4) University TV has been regarded as the most effective method of part-time education.
电视大学已经被认为是最有效的业余教育方法。

5) It has long been recognized as a beneficial practice to require students to wear school uniforms.
要求学生们穿校服一直被认为是一个有益的做法。

6) Young people should be encouraged to take part in more meaningful and valuable activities such as reading, studying and exercising.
年轻人应该被鼓励做更有意义、有价值的事情，如阅读、学习和锻炼。

7) We should compete for our survival, otherwise, we will be thrown out of the tide of society.
我们应该为生存而竞争，否则，我们会被社会潮流所淘汰。

XVII 疑问句和祈使句

1) However, can further scientific advance help the world solve the problem of future food supplies?
但是，人类是否能进一步借助科技进步来解决世界未来的粮食供应问题呢?

2) Is it a good phenomenon that pets enjoy better meals than some poor people?
宠物比一些穷人享用更好的饮食，这是好现象吗?

3) Then how should we treat these problems that came out of the urbanization?
那么，我们应该如何看待由城市化引起的诸多问题呢?

4) Since foreign languages have already been used as a tool in our daily life and machines cannot help us communicate completely, why do we give up studying foreign languages?
既然外语已作为一种工具为我们日常需要，既然机器无法帮助我们最大程度的实现沟通，我们还有什么理由放弃外语学习呢?

5) Let good advertisements facilitate communication between business people and the public, and help keep the business world moving.
让好的广告促进商人和公众之间的交流，并帮助商业界运行。

6) Never bring your work home. Leave it in your office.
永远不要将工作带回家。把它留在你的办公室。

第四章 句子改错

I 大小写

1. students should go abroad for study.

2. First of all, It can ensure the quality of university education.

II 标点符号

1. People have to devote more time and energy to their careers, some people are too occupied to spare time for their families.

2. Some people think that students should study abroad, other people believe that study abroad has some disadvantages.

3. This argument is true to some degree, however, I believe that students should study abroad.

4. Advertisements keep us well-informed about products, as a result, we can compare them and choose the best and cheapest one.

5. Advertisements keep us well-informed about products, in addition, we can find a job or rent a house with the help of advertisements.

III 名词单复数

1. In my opinion, student should study abroad.

2. Study abroad brings student a lot of benefit.

3. Going jogging is beneficial hobby which help people relax stress.

4. Sending child to go abroad is a luxurious dream for many poor family.

5. Playing PC game lavish parents' hard-earned money.

IV 时态和语态

1. Now more and more parents sent their children to study abroad.

2. Many companies are start to use Internet to train employees.

3. More and more children has been gone abroad to continue their study.

4. Citizen's rights to know truth should be respect

5. As is know to all, radio will not be replace by TV or internet.

6. With the opening up to the outside world, greater changes have been taken place in people's attitude towards family and marriage.

V 主谓不一致

1. My arguments is presented below.

2. Exploring the unknown places are a great pleasure to many people.

3. Rejecting the changes are unwise and passive.

4. Study abroad bring students a lot of benefits.

5. The problems which are brought about by raising pets is hard to resolve.

VI there be 句型使用错误

1. There are more and more people go abroad nowadays.

2. In nowadays, there is a great number of people choose to study abroad.

VII 动词短语做主语

1. Raise pets is becoming more and more popular.

2. It is commonly accepted that respect the old is a virtue.

3. The moral education plays an important role in bring families closer.

VIII 词性使用不当

1. It is benefit to children.

2. I am agree with the later view.

3. I think we should sending old people to nursing homes.

IX 代词使用错误

1. If one has talents and self-confidence, we will likely succeed.

2. If you try your best to practise more aerobic exercise, we can maintain good physical condition.

3. It is June now. Many students are busy preparing for the Entrance Examination to college. The great noise always makes him crazy.

4. The output of 1999 is more than 1998.

X 其他错误

1. The government will cost a large sum of money on the mass transit system.

2. It is a tough job to handle the question of youth drug abuse.

3. In my opinion, I think students should study abroad.

4. As the progress of the society, more and more peoples begin to be aware of the problem of …

5. As one of the most popularity thing is study abroad.

6. First of all, foreign countries, which create a wonderful language atmosphere for students.

一、大小写

1. Students should go abroad for study.

2. First of all, it can ensure the quality of university education.

二、标点符号

1. People have to devote more time and energy to their careers. Some people are too occupied to spare time for their families.
2. Some people think that students should study abroad. Other people believe that study abroad has some disadvantages.
3. This argument is true to some degree. However, I believe that students should study abroad.
4. Advertisements keep us well-informed about products. As a result, we can compare them and choose the best and cheapest one.
5. Advertisements keep us well-informed about products. In addition, we can find a job or rent a house with the help of advertisements.

三、名词单复数

1. In my opinion, students should study abroad.
2. Study abroad brings students a lot of benefits.
3. Going jogging is a beneficial hobby which helps people relaxes stress.
4. Sending children to go abroad is a luxurious dream for many poor families.
5. Playing PC games lavishes parents' hard-earned money.

四、时态和语态

1. Now more and more parents send their children to study abroad.
2. Many companies are starting to use Internet to train employees.
3. More and more children have gone abroad to continue their study.
4. Citizen's rights to know the truth should be respected.
5. As is known to all, radio will not be replaced by TV or internet.
6. With the opening up to the outside world, greater changes have taken place in people's attitude towards family and marriage.

五、主谓不一致

1. My arguments are presented below.
2. Exploring the unknown places is a great pleasure to many people.
3. Rejecting the changes is unwise and passive.
4. Study abroad brings students a lot of benefits.

5. The problems which are brought about by raising pets are hard to resolve.

六、there be 句型使用错误

1. There are more and more people going abroad nowadays.
2. Nowadays, there are a great number of people choosing to study abroad.

七、动词短语做主语

1. Raising pets is becoming more and more popular.
2. It is commonly accepted that respecting the old is a virtue.
3. The moral education plays an important role in bringing families closer.

八、词性使用不当

1. It is beneficial to children.
2. I agree with the later view.
3. I think we should send old people to nursing homes.

九、代词使用错误

1. If one has talents and self-confidence, he will likely succeed.
2. If we try our best to practise more aerobic exercise, we can maintain good physical condition.
3. It is June now. Many students are busy preparing for the Entrance Examination to college. The great noise always makes them crazy.
4. The output of 1999 is more than that of 1998.

十、其他错误

1. The government will spend a large sum of money on the mass transit system.
2. It is a tough job to handle the problem of youth drug abuse.
3. In my opinion, students should study abroad.
4. With the progress of the society, more and more people begin to be aware of the problem of …
5. One of the most popular things is study abroad.
6. First of all, foreign countries create a wonderful language atmosphere for students.

第五章　写作词汇

I Tourist 旅游类单词和短语

tour *n.* 旅游

tourism *n.* 旅游业

ecotourism *n.* 生态旅游业

place of interest/ sight/ resort *n.* 名胜，旅游度假胜地

appeal *v.* 吸引

attract *v.* 吸引

commercialize *v.* 商业化

over-commercialize *v.* 过度商业化

cultural invasion 文化上的入侵

local resident 本地居民

materialistic *adj.* 物质的

tertiary *adj.* 第三级的

tertiary industry *n.* 第三产业（服务业）

work exclusively for profit 唯利是图

money-worshipping 拜金的

broaden one's horizon 扩大某人的视野

enlarge one's vision 扩大某人的视野

enrich one's life 丰富某人的生活

interact *v.* 互动，交互影响

interaction *n.* 互动，交互影响

conflict *v.* 冲突

confliction *n.* 冲突

friction *n.* 摩擦，小冲突

heritage *n.* 遗产，继承物

legacy *n.* 祖先传下之物，遗赠物

first hand experience 直接经验
second hand experience 间接经验
take... as granted 认为……理所当然，想当然

II Finance 金融类单词和短语

boost *v.* 增加，支援，推进
curtail *v.* 缩减，简略
budget *n.* 预算；*v.* 节约开支
financial income 金融方面的收入
tax revenue 税收方面的收入
invest in... 投资于……
dedicate money to... 投资于……
allocate money to... 投资于……
expenditure *n.* 支出，消耗
cost *n.* 代价，付出；*v.* 花费，使付出
profit *n.* 利益；获利，*v.* 有益于
fund *n.* 基金；*v.* 为……提供资金
employment *n.* 雇佣
unemployment rate *n.* 失业率
employability skill 就业技能
laid-off workers 下岗职工
be reluctant to... 不情愿做……
financial turmoil 金融危机
financial crisis 金融危机
great depression 大萧条
globalization 全球化类单词和短语
cultural diversity 文化多样性
cultural integration 文化的整合
cross cultural 跨文化的
isolate *v.* 孤立，使孤立；*adj.* 孤立的
erode *v.* 侵蚀
destination *n.* 目的地

responsible *adj.* 负责的

responsibility *n.* 责任

civil *adj.* 文明的，公民的

civilize *v.* 使开化，使文明

civilization *n.* 文明，开化

global village 地球村

inspire *v.* 感动，激发

tradition *n.* 传统

traditional *adj.* 传统的

absorb *v.* 吸收，吸纳

diplomatic *adj.* 外交的，老练的

discord *n.* 分歧，不和谐；*v.* 不一致，不协调

dispute *n.* 争论；*v.* 争论，争执

polar *n.* 极性 n；*adj.* 两极的

polarize *v.* 使极化

polarization *n.* 极化

pivotal *adj.* 核心的，重要的

poverty *n.* 贫穷

famine *n.* 饥荒

pandemic *n.* （大范围流行的）疾病；*adj.* 全国流行的

labor pool 劳动人口库

recruit *n.* 招聘；*v.* 徽募

recruitment *n.* 征募

preserve *v.* 保存，保护

preservation *n.* 保存

protect *n.* 保护

ancestor *n.* 前辈

descendant *n.* 后代

ethnic minorities 少数民族

harmony *n.* 和谐

harmonious *adj.* 和谐的

evolve *v.* 进展，进化

evolving *adj.* 进展的，进化的

evolutionary *adj.* 进化的，发展的

revolutionary *adj.* 革命的
insular *adj.* 岛国的，狭隘的
provincial *adj.* 地方的，狭隘的
stable *adj.* 稳定的，可靠的
stability *n.* 稳定性

III Development 发展类的单词和短语

intensify *v.* 强化，加剧
strengthen *v.* 加强
magnify *v.* 放大，扩大
lessen *v.* 减少，变少
strengthen *v.* 加强
loosen *v.* 放松，松开
superior *n.* 上级；*adj.* 出众的
inferior *adj.* 次等的
productive *adj.* 多产的，有生产价值的
counterproductive *adj.* 反生产的，有碍生产力发展的
accelerate *v.* 加速
decelerate *v.* 减速
pace/tempo of life 生活节奏
obstruct *v.* 阻碍，妨碍
hinder *v.* 阻碍，妨碍
hamper *v.* 阻止，妨碍
impede *v.* 阻止，妨碍
exhaust *v.* 耗尽，使…精疲力竭
frustrate *v.* 挫败，打击
frustration *n.* 挫败感，令人沮丧的东西
fatigue *n.* 疲乏，疲劳；*v.* 使……疲劳
depress *v.* 使…沮丧
depression *n.* 沮丧，萧条
insomnia *n.* 失眠症
sleeplessness *n.* 失眠

rich *adj.* 富有的

wealthy *n.* 富人；*adj.* 富有的

well-off *adj.* 富有的

affluent *adj.* 富足的

poor *adj.* 贫穷的

impoverished *adj.* 赤贫的

destitute *adj.* 贫困的，赤贫的

indigent *adj.* 贫困的，贫穷的

needy *adj.* 贫穷的，贫困的

poverty *n.* 贫困，贫乏

alleviate *v.* 减轻，使……缓和

alleviation *n.* 减轻，缓和

disparity 不一致

break boundary between people 减少人和人之间的隔阂

eliminate 消除

create alienation between people 增加人和人之间的隔阂

reduce the disparity between the rich and the poor 降低贫富差距

infrastructure *n.* 基础设施

facilities *n.* 基本建设

public transport system 公共交通系统

water supply and drainage system 自来水给水排水系统

power grid 电网

pipe lines 疏通管道

IV City & Country 城市与乡村类单词和短语

skyscraper *n.* 摩天大楼

landline *n.* 风景线

urbanization *n.* 城市化

relocate *v.* 搬家，在配置

sedentary lifestyle 久坐不动的生活方式

function *n.* 功能；*v.* 功能

hypertension *n.* 高血压

heart disease 心脏病

excess nutrient 营养过剩

diabetes *n.* 糖尿病

obesity *n.* 肥胖症

cholesterol *n.* 胆固醇

traffic jams 交通阻塞

traffic congestion 交通阻塞

pedestrian *n.* 行人；*adj.* 徒步的，缺乏想象的

crosswalk *n.* 人行横道

jaywalk *v.* 乱闯马路

car accident 车祸

surveillance camera 监视摄像机

monitoring system 监视系统

spiritual life 精神生活

material life 物质生活

entertainment *n.* 娱乐

diversion *n.* 转移，娱乐活动

amuse *v.* 使……娱乐

amusement *n.* 娱乐

leisure *n.* 休闲

recreation *n.* 休闲，娱乐

V Population 人口相关的单词和短语

baby boom 婴儿潮

baby boomer 婴儿潮出生的人

population boom 人口迅速增长

population explosion 人口爆炸式增长

graying population 人口老龄化

birth control 节育

one child policy 独生子女政策

generation *n.* 代，一代

infant *n.* 婴儿；*adj.* 婴儿的，初具形态的

adolescent *n.* 青少年
young adult 年轻人
youth *n.* 年轻人
youngster *n.* 年轻人
elder *n.* 长者，长辈；*adj.* 年长的
elderly *adj.* 年长的

VI Architecture 建筑类的单词和短语

apartment *n.* 公寓
house *n.* 住宅；*v.* 居住，收容
complex *n.* 商住一体楼
concrete jungle 混凝土的丛林
folk house 民居
vernacular dwellings 民居
statue *n.* 雕塑
memorable *adj.* 值得纪念的，难忘的
for the sake of... 看在……的份上
building of historic importance 有特殊历史意义的建筑
building of special aesthetic value 有特殊审美价值的建筑
decrepit *adj.* 残破的，破旧的
creaky *adj.* 破烂的，吼吼嘎嘎的
wobbly *adj.* 摇摇欲坠的
raze a building 摧毁一栋楼
tear down 拆除，摧毁
knock down 拆除，摧毁

VII Environment 环境类的单词和短语

ecosystem *n.* 生态系统
wildlife *n.* 野生动植物
biota *n.* 生物系，动植物种类总称

biodiversity *n.* 生物多样性

ecological *adj.* 生态的，生态学的

balance *n.* 平衡

conserve 节约，保存

consume 消耗

deplete 耗尽，使……枯竭

use up 耗尽

damage *n.* 损害；*v.* 损坏

ruin *n.* 废墟，毁坏；*v.* 破坏，毁灭

deteriorate *v.* 恶化，使……恶化

aggravate *v.* 加剧，使……加剧

exploit *v.* 开发，利用

over-exploit *v.* 过度开发

utilize *v.* 利用，使用

reuse *v.* 再利用

recycle *v.* 回收

natural balance 自然平衡

natural resource 自然资源

renewable resource 可再生资源

disposable *adj.* 一次性的

non-renewable resource 不可再生资源

solar/tide/wind energy 太阳能/潮汐能/风能

petrol *n.* 汽油

metal *n.* 金属

mineral *n.* 矿产

fossil fuel 化石燃料

natural gas 天然气

coal *n.* 煤炭

shortage *n.* 短缺

scarcity *n.* 稀缺性

scarce *adj.* 稀缺的

sparse *adj.* 稀缺的，稀少的

ecological balance 生态平衡

sustainable *adj.* 可持续的

environmentalist 环保主义者

deforestation *n.* 沙漠化
forest logging 森林伐木
ozone layer 臭氧层
global warming 全球变暖
carbon dioxide 二氧化碳
acid rain 酸雨
pollute *v.* 污染
contaminate *v.* 污染
respiratory disease 呼吸道疾病
toxic *adj.* 有毒的
poisonous *adj.* 有毒的
vicious circle 恶性循环
discharge *v.* 排放
sewage *n.* 污水
gas waste 废气
inorganic trash 不可降解垃圾
agriculture *n.* 农业
farmland *n.* 农田
arable land 可耕地
crop yield 农作物产量
fertile soil 富饶的土壤
infertile soil 贫瘠的土壤

VIII Government 政府类相关的单词和短语

common people 普通老百姓
citizen *n.* 公民
transparent *adj.* 透明的
democratic *adj.* 民主的
democracy *n.* 民主
autocratic *adj.* 独裁的
progressive *adj.* 进步的
authority *n.* 权力机构

stringent 严格的

legislate *v.* 立法，制定法律

legislation *n.* 法规，法律

regulate *v.* 管理，调整

regulation *n.* 规章制度

administer *v.* 管理，执行

administration *n.* 管理，执行

prohibit *v.* 禁止

ban *v.* 禁止

scrutiny *n.* 审查，推敲

scrutinize *v.* 仔细检查

policy making 制定政策

myopic/near-sighted policy 缺乏远见卓识的政策

implement *v.* 实施，执行

execute *v.* 执行，实行

put...into practice 付诸……于实践

priority *n.* 优先，优先权

prioritize *v.* 给……以优先权

give priority to... 给……以优先权

aggressive *adj.* 强烈的，有进取心的，有攻击性的

expand *v.* 增加，扩展

expansion *n.* 扩展

national security 国家安全

arms *n.* 武器

armaments *n.* 武器

arm race 军备竞赛

space racc 航天竞赛

espionage *n.* 间谍行为

IX Crime 犯罪类的单词和短语

crime rate 犯罪率

violate/break the law 违法，犯法

comply with the law 遵纪守法

law-abiding citizens 遵纪守法的公民

perpetrator *n.* 犯法者

offender/ criminal *n.* 罪犯

drug smuggler 毒贩子

drug addict 瘾君子

inmate *n.* 囚犯

convict *n.* 罪犯；*v.* 宣判……有罪

commit *v.* 做…事（多指负面的），犯罪

heinous crime 重罪

felony *n.* 重罪

petty crime 轻罪

first time criminal 初犯者

repeat criminal 惯犯

tackle *v.* 处理，解决

solve *v.* 解决，处理

victim *n.* 受害者，牺牲

victimize *v.* 使…牺牲，使……受骗

justice *n.* 司法，正义，公正

be brought to justice 被绳之以法

law enforcement agencies 执法机关

punish *v.* 惩罚

punishment *n.* 惩罚

rampant 猖獗的

condemn *v.* 谴责

condone *v.* 宽恕

lenient *adj.* 宽大的，仁慈的

mercy *n.* 仁慈，宽恕；*adj.* 仁慈的，宽恕的

cruel *adj.* 残酷的，残忍的

brutal and cold blooded 惨无人道的

outrage *n.* 暴行；*v.* 激怒

outrageous *adj.* 过分的，令人发指的

track down 追查，追捕

hunt down 追查，追捕

imprison *v.* 监禁，束缚
console *v.* 安慰，慰藉
spiritual consolation 精神上的慰藉
deter potential crime 预防潜在的犯罪
be the exclusively causal factor of 唯一的决定因素
be the main culprit of 罪魁祸首
be the root of all evils 万恶之源

 Media 媒体类的单词和短语

popular *adj.* 流行的
prevalent *adj.* 流行的，普遍的
subjective *adj.* 主观的，有失偏颇的
objective *adj.* 客观的
bias *n.* 偏见；*v.* 使……偏心
biased *adj.* 有失偏颇的
celebrity *n.* 名人
entertain *v.* 娱乐
entertaining *adj.* 娱乐的
local/national/international/ news 本地/国家/国际 新
paparazzi *n.* 狗仔队
privacy *n.* 隐私
intrude one's privacy 侵犯他人隐私
fraudulent *adj.* 欺诈的，不诚实的
misleading *adj.* 有误导性的
distort *v.* 歪曲
distorted *adj.* 歪曲的
distortion 扭曲，变形
false *adj.* 虚假的
media hype 媒体炒作
exaggerate *v.* 夸大
exaggeration *n.* 夸张，夸大
trust worthy 值得信赖

dependable *adj.* 值得依赖

reliable *adj.* 可靠的，可信的

reliability *n.* 可靠性

code of ethics 道德准则

coverage *n.* 报道

press *n.* 压力；*v.* 按，压

news agencies 新闻机构

print media 平面媒体

new media 新兴媒体

informative *adj.* 信息量丰富的，见闻广博的

be flooded with 充斥着……

be saturated with 充斥着……

scandal *n.* 丑闻，耻辱

stain *n.* 污点；沾污

tarnish *n.* 污点；*v.* 沾污

reputation *n.* 声誉，好名声

fame *n.* 名声，声望

cover up *v.* 掩盖

gloss over *v.* 掩饰

censorship *n.* 审查制度

censor *v.* 审查

exclude *v.* 排除，拒绝

eliminate *v.* 除去，剔除

excise *v.* 除去，切除

XI Education 教育类的单词和短语

downgrade *v.* 批评，使降级

disparage *v.* 视，贬损

belittle *v.* 轻视，贬低

criticize *v.* 批评

critics *v.* 批评家，批评

discredit *n.* 失信；*v.* 损失信誉

praise *n.* 赞扬；*v.* 称赞，赞美
appreciate *v.* 欣赏，感激
acclaim *n.* 赞扬；*v.* 赞同
endorse *v.* 支持，赞同，代言
endorsement *n.* 支持；代言
compulsory education 义务教育
schooling *n.* 学校教育；学费
home-schooling 家庭教育
upbringing *n.* 教养
independent *adj.* 独立的，私立的
independent thinking 独立思考
obligation *n.* 义务，责任
sense of obligation 义务感
obligatory *adj.* 义务的
sedulous *adj.* 勤勉的
diligent *adj.* 勤勉的
hard-working *adj.* 勤勉的
endeavor *n.* 努力；*v.* 努力
talent *n.* 才能，天资
talented *adj.* 有才能的
creativity *n.* 创造力
creative *adj.* 创造性的
learn things by rote 机械式学习
learn things through understanding 理解式学习
force-feed *v.* 强行灌输
stifle/constrain creativity 扼杀创新能力
create *v.* 创造；*adj.* 创造的
create undue pressure 创造不必要的压力
peer pressure 来自同辈的压力
inspire *v.* 激发
inspiration *n.* 灵感
mental *adj.* 精神的
physical *adj.* 身体的
psychological *adj.* 心理的

moral *adj.* 道德上的；*n.* 品行

instill high moral value 灌输高尚的价值观

benefit *n.* 好处；*v.* 有益于

beneficial *adj.* 有益的

methodology *n.* 方法学

syllabus *n.* 摘要，大纲

curriculum *n.* 课程

extra-curricular activities 课外活动

discipline *n.* 学科，纪律

indiscipline *n.* 不规律

behavior *n.* 行为，举止

disruptive students 捣乱的学生

unruly students 难管教的学生

motivate *v.* 给予动机，激发

motivation *n.* 动机

cultivate *v.* 培养

cultivation *n.* 培养

foster *v.* 养育；*adj.* 养育的

adaptability *n.* 适应性

adapt to 适应

get accustomed to 适应

memorize *v.* 记录

apply *v.* 应用，申请

equation *n.* 方程

formula *n.* 公式

theorem *n.* 定理

enthusiasm *n.* 热情

enthusiastic *adj.* 热心的

follow ... blindly 盲从

critical thinking 批判性思考

encourage *v.* 鼓励

feedback *n.* 反馈

evaluate *v.* 评估

evaluation *n.* 估价

cooperation *n.* 合作
cooperative *n.* 合作社；*adj.* 合作的
team spirit 团队精神
experience *n.* 经验；经验
social experience 社会经验
situation *n.* 处境
circumstance *n.* 环境
optimistic *adj.* 乐观的
pessimistic *adj.* 悲观的
challenge *n.* 挑战；*v.* 挑战
wit *n.* 聪明才智
witty *adj.* 富于机智的，诙谐的
wisdom *n.* 智慧，学问
saving grace 可取之处
adversity *n.* 不幸，灾难
contribute *v.* 为…做贡献
contribution *n.* 贡献，捐款
universal language 通行语言
lingua franca 通用语言
primary/secondary/tertiary/-level education 初等/中等/高等教育

XII University Subjects 大学学科类的单词和短语

social science 社会科学
science *n.* 自然科学
engineering *n.* 工程学
arts *n.* 文科，人文科学
political science 政治学
basic science 基础科学
applied science 应用科学
computer science 计算机科学
civil engineering 土木工程
mechanical engineering 机械工程

financial engineering 金融工程
automation *n.* 自动化
history *n.* 历史
theoretical knowledge 理论知识
humanities *n.* 人文科学
chemistry *n.* 化学
math *n.* 数学
physics *n.* 物理学
economics *n.* 经济学
psychology *n.* 心理学
sociology *n.* 社会学
generalist *n.* 通才
specialist *n.* 专才
specialization *n.* 专门化
specialize *v.* 特殊化
major *v.* 主修；*n.* 主修科目
minor *v.* 辅修；*n.* 辅修科目

 XIII Technology 科技类的单词和短语

sweeping trend 横扫一切的趋势
advance *n.* 先进；*v.* 前进
advanced *adj.* 高级的，先进的
cutting edge 先进的，前沿的
leap *v.* 剧增，跳跃
soar *n.* 高扬；*v.* 快速增长
invention *n.* 发明
imagination *n.* 想象力
innovate *v.* 创新
innovation *n.* 革新
enhance *v.* 提高
transform *v.* 改变；*n.* 变形
information explosion 信息爆炸

overwhelming *adj.* 势不可挡
overwhelmingly *adv.* 压倒性的
epoch *n.* 时期，时代
era *n.* 时期，时代
age *n.* 时期，时代
proliferate *v.* 迅速扩散，激增
proliferation *n.* 增殖，激增
efficiency *n.* 效率
efficient *adj.* 高效率的
machinery *n.* 机器，机械
labor intense 劳动密集型
labor saving 人力节约
energy depending 能源依赖型
energy saving 能源节约型
biochemistry *n.* 生物化学
biotechnology *n.* 生物技术
nanotechnology *n.* 纳米技术
gene *n.* 基因
generic information 遗传信息
generic modification 转基因
generic modified 转基因的
telecommunication *n.* 远程通信
satellite *n.* 卫星
clone *n.* 克隆；*v.* 克隆
stem cell 干细胞

XIV Family 家庭类的单词和短语

discrimination *n.* 歧视
sex discrimination 性别歧视
age discrimination 年龄歧视
race discrimination 种族歧视
racist *n.* 种族歧视者

agist *n.* 年龄歧视者

sexist *n.* 性别歧视者

sexism *n.* 性别歧视主义

equal *adj.* 平等的

gender equality 男女平等

enlighten *v.* 启蒙，启发

an enlightened society 一个开明的社会

offspring *n.* 后代

generation gap 代沟

personality *n.* 个性

household *n.* 家庭

be tied down by ... 被某事束缚

childbearing *n.* 分娩；*adj.* 分娩的

child rearing/caring 照料小孩

pregnant *adj.* 怀孕的，富含的

pregnancy *n.* 怀孕

maternal instinct 母性本能

housework *n.* 家务

single parent household 单亲家庭

abuse *n.* 滥用；*v.* 滥用

abusive *adj.* 滥用的，虐待的

abusive behavior 虐待行为

mistreat *v.* 虐待

domestic *adj.* 家庭的；*n.* 佣人

violence *v.* 暴力，狂热

ungrateful/unthankful *adj.* 不知感恩的

XV Animals 动物类的单词和短语

humane *adj.* 人道的

inhumane *adj.* 无人情味的，薄情的

pet *n.* 宠物

accompany *v.* 陪伴

companion *n.* 同伴；*v.* 陪伴
habitat *n.* 栖息地
species *n.* 物种
poach *v.* 偷猎
endangered species 濒危物种
on the brim of extinction 处在灭绝的边缘
extinct *adj.* 灭绝的
preach *v.* 宣扬
advocate *v.* 提倡
vivisection *n.* 活体解剖
clinical trial 临床实验
anaesthetic *adj.* 麻醉的；*n.* 麻醉剂
pain *n.* 疼痛；使疼痛
painful *adj.* 痛苦的；*v.* 使疼痛
ease/relieve/alleviate one's pain 缓解某人的疼痛
replace *v.* 取代
replacement *n.* 接替者
substitute *n.* 代用品；*v.* 代替
substitution *n.* 替换

XVI 常用的形容词、副词短语

significant/crucial/pivotal/indispensable/substantial *adj.* 重要的
severe/grievous/serious *adj.* 情况严重的
ascending/growing/increasing *adj.* 上升的
descending/declining/decreasing *adj.* 下降的
soaring/surging *adj.* 快速上升的
plummeting/plunging *adj.* 快速下降的
ample/sufficient *adj.* 充足的，足够的
numerous/a great deal of/ an abundance of/ a considerable number of 大量的
persistent/sustaining/consecutive/continuous/successive *adj.* 持续的
a variety of/a great diversity of/all sorts of/ an assortment of/separate/multitude of 多种多样的
permanent/perpetual/sempiternal *adj.* 永久的

numerous/countless/exhaustless/inexhaustible *adj.* 无穷尽的
tremendous/infinite/considerable *adj.* 极大的，巨大的
exceeding/extreme/extraordinary/intense *adj.* 非常的，极度的
imperative/urgent *adj.* 紧急的
prominent/distinct/marked/remarkable/brilliant *adj.* 卓越的
meaningless/insignificant/nonsensical *adj.* 毫无意义的
excellent/exclusive/optimum/optimal/admirable *adj.* 优秀的，极好的
typical/representative/characteristic *adj.* 典型的
farseeing/sagacious/advisable *adj.* 有远见的
appropriate/opportune/relevant *adj.* 适当的
arduous/difficult/formidable *adj.* 辛苦的，费劲的
scrupulous/prudential/meticulous *adj.* 谨慎的，认真的
miserable/painful *adj.* 痛苦的，悲惨的
empty/vacuous/blank/inane/vain *adj.* 空的，空虚的
presumptuous/unadvisable/ignorant *adj.* 不明智的
inapposite/incongruous/inappropriate *adj.* 不合适的，不适宜的
immutable/unchangeable *adj.* 不可改变的
inevitable/unavoidable/ineluctable *adj.* 不可避免的
undeniable *adj.* 不能否认的
irreparable/ irreversible *adj.* 不可挽回的
ordinarily/usually/commonly/generally *adv.* 一般地
for the time being/for a while/temporarily/transitorily 暂时地
constantly/continuously/in succession 连续地
extremely/extraordinarily *adv.* 非常地
especially/ particularly *adv.* 尤其地，特别地
certainly /definitely/undoubtedly/indeed/inevitably *adv.* 必然地
ultimately /eventually *adv.* 最终地
exclusively/merely/just *adv.* 仅仅地

第六章 模板式句型

I 辩论型题目 一边倒结构

1. 开头段介绍双方观点

Some / Many / Most / A majority of / Quite a few / A sizable percentage of people assert / contend / argue / hold / insist / maintain / claim / suggest / think / believe / proclaim / advocate / hold the view / hold the opinion / are confident / are of the opinion / have the idea / point out / take the view that ________. Others / Other people / Some others / Some other people assert / contend / argue / hold / insist / maintain / claim / suggest / think / believe / proclaim / advocate / hold the view / hold the opinion / are confident / are of the opinion / have the idea / point out / take the view that ________.

Some / Many / Most / A majority of / Quite a few / A sizable percentage of people assert / contend / argue / hold / insist / maintain / claim / suggest / think / believe / proclaim / advocate / hold the view / hold the opinion / are confident/are of the opinion / have the idea / point out / take the view that ________. But / However / Nevertheless / On the other hand, there are also some / many / most / a majority of / quite a few / a sizable percentage of people who (strongly / firmly) assert / contend / argue / hold / insist / maintain / claim / suggest / think / believe / proclaim / advocate / hold the view / hold the opinion / are confident / are of the opinion / have the idea / point out / take the view that ________.

Some / Many / Most / A majority of / Quite a few / A sizable percentage of people assert / contend / argue / hold / insist / maintain / claim / suggest / think / believe / proclaim / advocate / hold the view / hold the opinion / are confident / are of the opinion / have the idea / point out / take the view that ________, while / but / whereas others assert / contend / argue / hold / insist / maintain / claim / suggest / think / believe / proclaim / advocate/ hold the view / hold the opinion / are confident / are of the opinion / have the idea / point out / take the view that ________.

Some / Many / Most / A majority of / Quite a few / A sizable percentage of people assert / contend / argue / hold / insist / maintain / claim / suggest / think / believe / proclaim / advocate / hold the view / hold the opinion / are confident / are of the opinion / have the idea / point out / take the view that ________. But / However / Nevertheless / On the other hand, towards the same issue, many others assert / contend / argue / hold / insist / maintain / claim / suggest / think / believe / proclaim / advocate / hold the view / hold the opinion / are confident / are of the opinion / have the idea / point out / take the view that ________.

Some / Many / Most / A majority of / Quite a few / A sizable percentage of people assert / contend / argue / hold / insist / maintain / claim / suggest / think / believe / proclaim / advocate / hold the view / hold the opinion / are confident / are of the opinion / have the idea / point out / take the view that ________. But / However / Nevertheless / On the other hand, other people stand on a very different ground. They assert / contend / argue / hold / insist / maintain / claim / suggest / think / believe / proclaim / advocate / hold the view / hold the opinion / are confident / are of the opinion / have the idea / point out / take the view that ________.

Some / Many / Most / A majority of / Quite a few / A sizable percentage of people tend to assert / contend / argue / hold / insist / maintain / claim / suggest / think / believe / proclaim / advocate / hold the view / hold the opinion / are confident / are of the opinion / have the idea / point out / take the view that ________. But / However / Nevertheless / On the other hand, others assert / contend / argue / hold / insist / maintain / claim / suggest / think / believe / proclaim / advocate / hold the view / hold the opinion / are confident / are of the opinion / have the idea / point out / take the view that ________.

Some / Many / Most / A majority of / Quite a few / A sizable percentage of people assert / contend / argue / hold / insist / maintain / claim / suggest / think / believe / proclaim / advocate / hold the view / hold the opinion / are confident / are of the opinion / have the idea / point out / take the view that ________. Others, however / nevertheless / on the other hand, assert / contend / argue / hold / insist / maintain / claim / suggest / think / believe / proclaim / advocate / hold the view / hold the opinion / are confident / are of the opinion /

have the idea / point out / take the view that ________. Which you prefer depends on your own experience, life style and emotional concern.

2. 开头段介绍对方观点及其一到两个理由

Some / Many / Most / A majority of / Quite a few / A sizable percentage of people assert / contend / argue / hold / insist / maintain / claim / suggest / think / believe / proclaim / advocate / hold the view / hold the opinion / are confident / are of the opinion / have the idea / point out / take the view that__________. They assert / contend / argue / hold / insist / maintain / claim / suggest / think / believe / proclaim / advocate / hold the view / hold the opinion / are confident / are of the opinion / have the idea / point out / take the view that__________.

Some / Many / Most / A majority of / Quite a few / A sizable percentage of people assert / contend / argue / hold / insist / maintain / claim / suggest / think / believe / proclaim / advocate / hold the view / hold the opinion / are confident / are of the opinion / have the idea / point out / take the view that__________. They assert / contend / argue / hold / insist / maintain / claim / suggest / think / believe / proclaim / advocate / hold the view / hold the opinion / are confident / are of the opinion / have the idea / point out / take the view that__________. This argument is true to some degree.

Some / Many / Most / A majority of / Quite a few / A sizable percentage of people assert / contend / argue / hold / insist / maintain / claim / suggest / think / believe / proclaim / advocate / hold the view / hold the opinion / are confident / are of the opinion / have the idea / point out / take the view that__________. They assert / contend / argue / hold / insist / maintain / claim / suggest / think / believe / proclaim / advocate / hold the view / hold the opinion / are confident / are of the opinion / have the idea / point out / take the view that__________.There is no denying that there is some truth in the above point of view.

3. 开头段说出自己的观点

In my opinion, ______________.

As far as I am concerned, ______________.

As for me, ______________.

In/For my part, ______________.

In/From my point of view, ______________.

As I see it, ________________.

From my own perspective, ________________.

Speaking for myself, ________________.

I am convinced that ________________.

I would point out that ________________.

It seems quite clear to me that ________________.

For my part, I absolutely/wholeheartedly/totally/completely agree with/approve of/consent to/am for/share/side with the latter point of view.

There is probably a little bit of truth in both arguments. For my part, I absolutely/wholeheartedly/totally/completely agree with/approve of/consent to/am for/share/side with the latter one.

For my part, I absolutely/wholeheartedly/totally/completely agree with/approve of/consent to/am for/share/side with the former point of view.

4. 开头段引起下文

The reasons are presented below.

There are many reasons supporting my view.

There are no less than three reasons as rendered below.

There are many reasons that can verify this.

I support this with the following reasons.

I would like to present two explanations to confirm that I am right.

There are three advantages as follows.

A number of causes account for my point.

The reasons are chiefly as follows.

I believe that I have found some solid reasons.

There are numerous reasons why I hold this opinion, and I would explore a few of the most important ones here.

Among countless factors which influence my decision, there are two/three conspicuous aspects.

My arguments for this point are listed as follows.

This view is based on the propensity of following points.

There are three premier causes as follows.

This quite different view is based on the propensity of following points.

5. 第一个理由段主题句

The first reason that can be seen by every person is that__________________.

The main reason is that _______.

One very strong argument is that _______.

The reasons are quite clear. Above all, _______.

The most important benefit is that _______.

The main reason why _______ is that _______.

The first reason can be seen by every person. __________________.

First, we can observe easily that_______.

The first and most important reason is that _______.

I agree with the above statement because I believe that _______.

One of the reasons is that _______.

Perhaps this is because of the simple fact that _______.

One of the most important things is that _______.

One of the primary causes is that _______.

I agree with the statement without reservation since _______.

We cannot forget a universal truth that__________________.

Beyond enormous obvious reasons, there lies a more in-depth cause. __________________.

My first reason for this is that__________________.

One of the most attractive points is that _______.

Certainly no other reason in my decision is more crucial than the one as follow.__________________.

In term of substantive level, the reason mentioned below seems to be advisable and deserve more consideration. ____________________________.

The main reason for my propensity is that _______.

We may look into every possible reason; however, foremost reason for this is that_______.

First,

Firstly,

First of all,

To begin with,

In the first place,

On the one hand,

First and foremost,

For one thing,

6. 第二个理由段主题句

Another factor that we must consider is that ________.

It might also be noted that ________.

There is a further more subtle point we must consider. ________.

Another reason why I agree with the above statement is that I believe ________.

What is also worth noticing is that ________.

Another reason why I prefer the argument is that ________.

There is another factor that deserves some words here. ________.

A more essential factor why I advocate the argument is that ________.

Another reason why I advocate the attitude is that ________.

A further reason why I prefer the argument is that ________.

Another benefit is that ________.

The second reason for my propensity is that ________.

Another factor shows that ________.

The second thing that must be taken into consideration is that ________.

Perhaps another reason lies in the fact that ________.

Another factor that should be taken into consideration is that ________.

Second,

Secondly,

Next,

Besides,

In the second place,

For another,

Furthermore,

Moreover,

In addition,

What is more,

More important, ________.

7. 第三个理由段主题句

The third and very important reason is that ________.

Finally, the incomparable advantage of this view is that ________.

Finally,

Third,

Thirdly,

Furthermore,

Moreover,

In addition, _______.

What is more, _______.

More important, _________________.

Most important, _________________.

Last but not least, _______.

Some people may say that ___________________. In fact, __________________.

Of course, _____________________. However, __________________________.

We must admit that ____________________________. However, it cannot be denied that ________________.

As a matter of fact, ____________________. However, we also cannot deny that _______.

8. 结尾段第一句

From what has been discussed above, we may safely draw the conclusion that ______.

So, as I see it, _______.

So from what has been discussed, one can reach only this conclusion: ____________.

After understanding the reasons above, it is quite safe now to say that ____________.

Now, after close examination, it is not difficult to draw the conclusion that ________.

So if we take a careful consideration, it is not difficult to get the conclusion: ________.

So, based on the above discussion, I agree with the opinion that _______.

Once you have known all of these, you must agree with me that ______________.

Based on the above discussion and analysis, we can see that _______.

From what has been discussed above, I think the correct attitude is that _______.

From what has been stated above, I suppose that _______.

All the above reasons suggest that we can come to the simple conclusion that _______.

To sum up, I firmly commit to the notion that _______.

To sum up, I feel that, overall, there are strong positive effects of _______.

To sum up, it is obvious for us to conclude that _______.

To sum up, there is no question in my mind that _______.

All in all, I should say that _______.

To sum up/In general/Generally/In brief/In sum/In conclusion/In short/In a word, _______.

Taking into all these factors, we may reasonably come to the conclusion that _______.

From what has been discussed above, we may safely arrive at the conclusion that _______.
Therefore, it is not difficult for us to come to the conclusion that _______.
From what has been mentioned above, we can clearly see that _______.
Consequently, I strongly commit to the notion that _______.
From what has been discussed above, I strongly approve of the notion that _______.
Judging from all evidence offered, we may reasonably come to the conclusion that _______.
For the reasons presented above, I strongly commit to the notion that _______.
All the evidence justifies an unshakable view that _______.
All the evidence supports an unmistakable conclusion that _______.
Taking into account of all these factors, we may reach the conclusion that _______.
All reliable evidences point to one saying, that is _______.
For the reasons presented above, I strongly commit to the notion that _______.
Given the factors I have just outlined, I can only say that _______.
To sum up, it is sagacious to support the statement that _______.

II 辩论型题目 对称式结构

1. 开头段介绍双方观点

2. 开头段引起下文

It is quite understandable that people from different backgrounds put different interpretations on the same issue.
Admittedly, there are merits to both arguments.
Admittedly, there are merits to both sides of the argument.
Admittedly, both sides are reasonable.
It is quite natural that people from different backgrounds may have divergent attitudes towards it.
Both sides have their merits.
Both sides of the argument have very strong feelings and sound reasons.
Both sides of the question are well supported by sound reasons.
Before giving my opinion, I think it is important to look at the argument on both sides.
Before rendering my opinion, I think it is important to take a glance at the arguments on

both sides.

Views on this issue vary from person to person.

It is quite natural that people seldom reach a total agreement on such a long-running controversy.

People rarely reach an absolute consensus on such a controversial issue.

Undeniable, there are points in both sides of the argument.

People's views, however, are divergent on the matter in question.

This issue is so controversial that people can hardly reach an absolute consensus.

This is a very controversial issue and people hold quite different opinions of it.

There are people on both sides of the argument who have very strong feelings.

It is quite understandable that views on this issue vary from person to person.

On such a controversial issue, people seldom reach an absolute consensus.

This is a controversial issue, which often arouses heated discussions among people.

Nevertheless, people seldom reach an absolute consensus on such a controversial issue.

Both sides are supported by good reasons.

There are advantages and disadvantages on both sides.

There are people on both sides of the argument who have very strong feelings.

There are different views concerning this topic.

Both patterns present advantages and disadvantages.

People rarely reach an absolute consensus on such a controversial issue.

On such a controversial issue, people seldom reach an absolute consensus.

This issue is so controversial that people can hardly reach an absolute consensus.

This is a very controversial issue and people hold quite different opinions of it.

It is quite natural that people seldom reach a total agreement on such a long-running controversy.

Both sides of the question are well supported by sound reasons.

People from different backgrounds would put different interpretations on the same case.

3. 第二段第一句

Those who believe that____________give their reasons as follows.

People, who advocate that _______, have their sound reasons.

Some people are of the opinion that_______________.

People who support that ______ give some of the following reasons.

There are several reasons which suggest that _______.

There are several reasons why ________.

There are some major causes why________________.

Many people argue that ________.

Those people who strongly believe that ______ have cogent reasons for it.

On the one hand, some people suggest that________________.

Some arguments can be made that ________________.

4. 第三段第一句

However, the other side of the coin voices its strong opposition, saying that________.

On this issue, some other people hold a different attitude, arguing that____________.

People rarely reach an absolute consensus on such a controversial issue. The other side of the coin has voiced strong opposition, saying that________________________.

However, there are also some others who contend that_______.

However, there are a large number of people who hold a different view concerning this case. They believe that________________.

On the other hand, some other people strongly against the above attitude. In their view,____________.

However, views on this issue vary from person to person. Some people believe that____________.

There is no denying that there is some truth in the above point of view. However, to some people's mind, ____________.

Other people's opinion is just the opposite. They strongly believe that __________.

Inevitably, on the other side, there are others who strongly advocate that _______.

But other people set forth a totally different argument about this case. They contend that_________.

Some people examine this issue from another angle. They claim that__________.

On the other hand, there are also many opponents who strongly argue that______.

However, further analysis would make it clear that ________________________.

5. 第四段第一句

There is probably a little bit of truth in both arguments. For my part, I completely agree with the latter view that________________.

It is quite understandable that people from different backgrounds put different interpretations on the same issue. For my part, I stand on the latter opinion that____________________.

Admittedly, there are merits to both arguments. As far as I am concerned, I firmly commit to the notion that________________.

From the above comparison and contrast, anyone can safely conclude that _______.

With views of both sides considered, I think that _______.

Both sides make sense. Therefore it is really hard for me to draw a definite conclusion. To my mind, _______.

Both sides above make sense, and consequently it is hard to come to an absolute conclusion. In my opinion, _______.

Admittedly, both sides are reasonable. But they are one-sided. In my opinion, _______.

As far as I am concerned, I think there is truth in the argument of these two parties. As for me, _______________________.

To sum up, we cannot deny that both sides are well-grounded. In my opinion, _______.

Both opinions make sense, and consequently it is hard to decide which one is more reasonable. From my own perspective,____________________.

From what has been mentioned above, we may see that there is some truth in both arguments. Personally, I side with the latter opinion that______________.

So, based on the above discussion, I agree with the opinion that _______.

Once you have known all of these, you must agree with me that _______________.

Based on the above discussion and analysis, we can see that _______.

Taking into account both sides of argument, I think _______.

In my opinion, I would point out that________________.

As for me, I am convinced that________________.

As far as I am concerned, I strongly believe that________________.

In/From my point of view, I support that________________.

As I see it, I am in favor of the latter point of view that________________.

From my own perspective, ________________.

Speaking for myself, ________________.

III 解释型题目 基本同一边倒结构

1. 开头段最后一句

What factors lead to this phenomenon and what we can do to solve the problem has become a concern to many people. In my opinion, the following reasons should be taken into consideration.

It is crucial that we analyze the causes of this disturbing issue and explore effective solutions. From my own perspective, the causes are multiple.

It is not easy to render the reasons for this complicated phenomenon which involves several factors.

In my mind, the following factors need to be taken into consideration.

There are several reasons for this phenomenon.

There are several reasons for this problem.

The causes may be inner and outer influence.

There are a number of reasons for this phenomenon.

Hence, it is imperative that we pinpoint the causes of this disturbing phenomenon.

2. 两/三个原因段的第一句

3. 结尾段第一句

This issue should be well taken into consideration. As for how to address the problem, people put forward various suggestions.

Regarding these reasons, I think there are some ways to deal with the problem. In order to solve the problem, people set forth different solutions and here I would explore only two key ways.

I strongly suggest that effective steps be taken as soon as possible to address the problem.

The following suggestions should be taken into consideration when we are seeking solutions to cope with the problem.

Considering the severity of this issue, we have no choice but to take stringent measures to address this problem.

We should take effective measures to solve the problem.

It is crucial that we take vigorous measures to tackle these problems.

Given the severity of this phenomenon, we have no alternative/option but to take immediate/prompt steps to address this situation.

In view of the seriousness of this problem, effective measures must be taken before things get worse.

IV 解释型题目 基本同对称式结构

1. 第二段第一句

The following reasons should be taken into consideration.

It is not easy to render the reasons for this complicated phenomenon which involves several factors.

The following factors need to be taken into consideration.

There are several reasons for this phenomenon.

There are several reasons for this problem.

The causes may be inner and outer influence.

There are a number of reasons for this phenomenon.

The causes are multiple.

From my own perspective, the causes of this phenomenon are manifold.

It is imperative that we pinpoint the causes of this disturbing phenomenon.

2. 第三段第一句

This issue should be well taken into consideration. As to how to address the problem, people put forward various suggestions.

Regarding these reasons, I think there are some ways to deal with the problem.

In order to solve the problem, people set forth different solutions and here I would explore only two key ways.

I strongly suggest that effective steps be taken as soon as possible to address the problem.

The following suggestions should be taken into consideration when we are seeking solutions to cope with the problem.

Considering the severity of this issue, we have no choice but to take stringent measures to address this problem.

We should take effective measures to solve the problem.

It is crucial that we take vigorous measures to tackle these problems.

Given the severity of this phenomenon, we have no alternative but to take immediate steps to address this situation.

In view of the seriousness of this problem, effective measures must be taken before things get worse.

3. 第四段

There are many reasons which result in this unpleasant phenomenon and something should be done as soon as possible to solve the problem.

In short, this disturbing problem is attributed to many factors and I believe with the joint efforts from individuals and the government, it can be eventually resolved.

1. 辩论型题目一边倒结构完整模板样例

(________________.) Some people suggest that________. Other people advocate that________. For my part, I absolutely agree with the latter point of view. (The reasons are presented below.)

The first reason that can be seen by every person is that________________. ______________.__________________.________________.

Another factor that we must consider is that________.________.________.________.

The third and very important reason is that ________.________.______________.______ ______.

或者:

Some people may say that________________. In fact,________________. ____________.____________.

From what has been discussed above, we may safely draw the conclusion that ______. (__________.______________. What is more,______________.)

2. 辩论型题目一边倒结构开头段写法二

(______________________.) A sizable percentage of people hold the opinion that________________. They claim that______________. This argument is true to some degree. However, I am convinced that____________. (The reasons are presented below.)

3. 辩论型题目对称式结构完整模板样例

(________________.) Some people suggest that__________. Other people advocate that__________. It is quite understandable that people from different backgrounds put different interpretations on the same issue.

Those who believe that_____________give their reasons as follows. In the first place, _________._________.In the second place,_____________.________________. Furthermore, ______________.____________________.

However, the other side of the coin voices its strong opposition, saying that________.For one thing,________________.___________________. For another,_______________._____________. In addition,_____________._________________.

There is probably a little bit of truth in both arguments. For my part, I completely agree with the latter view that_______________.______________.________________.________________.

4. 解释型题目基本同一边倒结构完整模板样例

___________________________________. _____________________________________. What factors lead to this phenomenon and what we can do to solve the problem has become a concern to many people. In my opinion, the following reasons should be taken into consideration.

The first reason that can be seen by every person is that______________________. ________________._____________________.___________________.

Another factor that we must consider is that__________.__________.___________._________.

The third and very important reason is that ________.___________.________________.______ ________.

This issue should be well taken into consideration. As to how to address the problem, people put forward various suggestions. In the first place, _______________________. In the second place,_____________. In addition, _________________.

5. 解释型题目基本同对称式结构完整模板样例

____________________________________. _____________________________________.

The following reasons should be taken into consideration. The first reason is that__________ _____._______________. Another reason is that_____________._____________. Furthermore, _____________.________________.

This issue should be well taken into consideration. As to how to address the problem, people put forward various suggestions. In the first place,____________. ___________. In the second place,_____________. ______________.In addition, _________________. _____________.

There are many reasons which result in this unpleasant phenomenon and something should be done as soon as possible to solve the problem.

SUMMARY

第七章 常见考试话题观点范例

Topic 1: Advertisements should be restricted or not

1. Advertisements provide us with much useful information. Advertisements keep us well-informed about products. As a result, we can compare them and choose the best and cheapest one. In addition, we can find a job or rent a house with the help of advertisements.
2. Advertisements bring us a lot of entertainment. We cannot imagine what a bus station or a newspaper would be like without advertisements. Would you enjoy watching a blank wall or reading traffic regulations while waiting for a bus? An interesting advertisement makes your waiting less dull and monotonous.
3. Advertisements also provide money for newspapers, magazines, radios and TV stations. Many kinds of media could not survive without advertisements. Because of advertising, we can enjoy so many TV programs with so little money. A newspaper will cost much more if we have to pay its full price.

Topic 2: Study abroad

Advantages:

1. Overseas study can broaden one's horizons. The knowledge of social customs acquired in the other countries helps one to become more open-minded.
2. Students can learn advanced science and technology. They have easy access to the first-rate facilities and the latest development in science and technology.
3. Studying abroad is a good way for one to cultivate independence. One has to learn how to take care of and protect oneself, and how to get on well with people from different cultural backgrounds.

4. One can attain a good command of a foreign language. Studying abroad provides a wonderful language environment for students.
5. When one finishes his study abroad, he will have more choices for his future career. It is conducive to one's self-betterment and self-realization.
6. By looking at one's own country from the outside, one can best see the strengths and weaknesses of one's motherland. Many people who have lived in other countries feel that the experience enables them to understand their own country better.

Disadvantages:

1. Living far away from home, students often suffer from psychological problems such as loneliness and homesickness. Some of them may even fail to adapt themselves to the overseas life till the end of their study.
2. Many students do not want to return to their native country after graduation because most of them want to seek a more comfortable life and a brighter future. This may result in a serious brain-drain and our country will inevitably cause a huge loss of talent.
3. Studying abroad lays a great financial burden on the students' family. The tuition fee is costly and living expenses are much higher. It is not easy for ordinary students to cover high college cost.
4. They find it hard to follow teachers and native speakers because of the language barrier. It will bring them inconvenience in their studies.
5. When returning to one's motherland, one may suffer from the so-called reverse culture shock.
6. Without their parents' supervision, some overseas students tend to ignore their studies.

Topic 3: Families are not as close as before

Causes:

1. People face fierce competition and suffer from great pressure. One has to work and study hard to meet the demand of society. People have to devote more time and energy to their careers and they have to broaden their scope of knowledge constantly. Some people are too occupied to spare time for their families.
2. There are more forms of entertainment available. High technology brings modern people more interesting things which can easily attract their attention, such as TV, the

Internet and PC games. They are addicted to these activities, totally neglecting the feelings of other family members.

3. People are now more independent than before. Apart from their family, they can easily get help from their friends. It is much easier to make more friends now as a result of the rapid improvement in telecommunication. Therefore they are not as dependent on their families as before.

Solutions:

1. We should spare more time with our families no matter how occupied we are. Try to squeeze some time for a regular family dinner because dinner is a perfect time and opportunity for people to exchange their feelings and ideas.
2. Teach the children a sense of family when they are still young in order to form good habits like writing letters and making telephone calls to each other. When they are out, we should remind them that they should call home regularly.
3. It is the government's responsibility to organize activities to promote public awareness of the importance of a harmonious family relationship. The government should give awards to some happy families in recognition of their striving for a better family relationship.

Topic 4: Advantages and disadvantages of city life

Advantages:

1. Every year men and women crowd into cities in search of employment and a decent living. There are more job opportunities in the city and city dwellers earn more money. As far as meals and clothes are concerned, urban citizens are well fed and well dressed as there is an adequate supply of goods.
2. Urban citizens can appreciate a more colorful life than rural citizens. The city provides a lot of places for entertainment. Living in the country lacks entertainment.
3. Some people prefer to live in big cities because big cities offer more conveniences than small towns. Shopping, a necessary activity in everyday life is more convenient in the city than in the country. Townspeople can buy what they want at any time of a day. But rural residents go to town at most once a week. Urban traffic is so well developed that the residents there often visit exhibitions and parks which are only a short bus ride away. For country people this is an operation which involves considerable planning.

4. City dwellers are well informed because they have the easier access to news. But rural residents are too busy to pay particular attention to them. It is for these reasons that more and more people are pilling into the city and looking for a nest there. For every one who moves out at least ten are waiting to come in.

Disadvantages:

1. One big problem is the ever-increasing pressure produced by over-crowding. Cities have been exposed not only to the problem of traffic and housing, but also to the problem of education, sanitation, employment and so on. It takes ages for a bus to get to you. Even when a bus does at last arrive, it's so full that it cannot take any more passengers.
2. Another is the growing number of cars and buses, whose exhaust sends huge quantities of carbon dioxide into the atmosphere, making the air of cities unbreathable.
3. City dwellers lose touch with nature. A few flowers in a public park, if you have time to visit it, may remind you that it is spring or summer. A few leaves clinging to the pavement may remind you that it is autumn.
4. You pay dearly for the privilege of living in a city. The demand for accommodation is so great that it is often impossible for ordinary people to buy a house of their own. Costly rents must be paid for tiny flats which even country hens would disdain to live in. Everything you buy is likely to be more expensive than it would be in the country.
5. The most serious and pressing problem is the widespread crime. Bank robberies which were unheard of in the past now occur more frequently. Today, even walking in the street in the day will make you nervous, let alone in the late night. City-dwellers live under constant threat. The crime rate in most cities is very high. All these problems make big cities no longer attractive to people as years before. Only a madman would choose to live in a large modern city.

Topic 5: Advantages and disadvantages of modern technology

Advantages:

1. Science has changed so much of today's world. Due to science, we now live safer, more comfortable and convenient lives.
2. We all hope that modern technology will reach a higher level, because modern technology makes life more convenient indeed.

3. Modern technology makes life more convenient; tools are the milestones of the technology as well as human being's progress. Men used to cut trees with hand saw. But now, by using electronic saw they can cut down a tree in only a few minutes.
4. Another example is more vivid: You have something urgent which has to be informed to your friend whose house is two hour's ride away. You probably want to make a phone call. But no telephone is installed in your friend's home. What could you do?
5. For example, much of the heavy work which used to be done by hand has now been fulfilled by automatic machines, efficient robots and powerful computers.
6. Man can, nowadays, travel to the far corners of the world and even land on the moon.
7. The vast improvements made in the field of medicine have served to lengthen our life expectancy and to reduce the rate of infant mortality. Medical breakthroughs have eradicated many fatal diseases that were once common. Better health also helps people prevent slowly debilitating conditions, such as heart disease, which can take their lives at an early age.
8. As civilization has advanced, our living environment and sources of food have become more sanitary.
9. The discovery of mechanization, better seeds, better techniques of irrigation and pest control have worked to increase productivity levels on farms.
10. In transportation, the railway, modern ocean liner, jet plane, and motor vehicle have made our lives more comfortable and provided great possibilities for modern commercial development and industrialization.

Disadvantages:

1. In the modern life of ours, it is ironic that we find ourselves being more and more enslaved by science instead of being freed by it.
2. Now we are so dependent on the products of science that we cannot imagine how we could go on living without them.
3. However, science has been responsible for pollution and has given us the nuclear bomb which threatens our very existence. Worst of all, high-tech has created all kinds of deadly weapons such as nuclear missiles.
4. Modern industry, as well as modern traffic conveniences, has created a serious problem of air pollution. The "green house effect" is now threatening the existence of mankind.
5. Some ethicists regard the cloning of humans as a morally unjustifiable intrusion into human life. The cloning is a remarkable breakthrough in bioengineering. But it soon caused worldwide concern over its ethical, social and scientific implications.

Topic 6: Advantages and disadvantages of the computer

Advantages:

1. At the time the computer was invented, scientists, carried away (使激动，兴奋) by its calculating speed, felt that they had created a miracle. It was gradually used not only in mathematics, physics, chemistry and astronomy, but in places like the library, hospital and military army to replace the works of man. Somehow, computer is no longer patent of professional computer engineers. More and more common people even pupils can use computers in their daily life.
2. Conquering the universe, discovering new things, and explaining mysterious phenomena puzzling us at present are all made possible by computer.
3. Computers take over routine jobs in the office and at home. Today we can say for sure that computers have entered thousands of families.
4. At the present time, there is a great deal of interest in the use of computers in education.
5. IT industry plays a more and more important role in the modern social activities. Communication with computers is fast and easy.

Disadvantages:

1. In other aspects, computer affects people's daily life and do harm to people. There are many people lost themselves in Internet and the worse, they commit crimes by Internet.
2. Nearly all the people, from pupils to the old, can get the harm from computer more or less. For this reason, computer should be banned from people's lives.
3. If we depend on modern technology too much, it will bring bad effects especially to children.
4. During the growth of children, basic education is essential. Computers and scientific tools should not replace school education.
5. Through systematic study in school, children can learn how to study, how to create and how to be a human being. But through computer, children can only learn how to oversimplify the life. In this way, children will become very lazy and unwilling to use their mind.
6. Since computers are convenient, there is a new challenge to primary school teachers: pupils can use computer or scientific calculator in the class of grammar and mathematics instead of doing those coalitions by their own brains. By this children can work out problems quickly but what they have learned is just typing skill not

mathematics skill, so I think computer should be banned in class.

7. Besides, staying in front of the computer to long will be detrimental to children's health. The radiation from the computer will arise many uncomfortable feelings. For instance, losing hair, not sleeping very well and having a headache, etc..
8. The biggest harm to children is that staring at the computer for a long time will damage the vision. So the children have to wear a pair of glasses early from their school days. It will do harm to the whole process of their growth.
9. At the same time, they will reduce the amount of exercise.
10. This kind of dependence on computer also can arise the dependence on their parents in life. If they do their homework with easy tools, how can they do their own businesses through themselves? They may just sit in front of the computer and ask for this and that without moving.

Topic 7: Private cars

Advantages:

1. With the increase of our nation's economic power, cars are increasingly entering families, and the popularization of cars is widely taken as the sign of modernization.
2. It is true that the whole world is witnessing China's construction of modernization. Comparing China with the western countries, many people hold that it is quite necessary for China to build a powerful car industry in the course of modernization.
3. And in many cities, the popularization of private cars is viewed as an important sign of local economic growth.
4. Before the automobile, goods and people were often transported by train or horse-drawn wagon.
5. The trains did not run everywhere and horses were slow and could carry only limited loads.
6. The automobile made it possible for people to travel door-to-door at a reasonable speed and in relative comfort.
7. Traveling was no longer a time-consuming, uncomfortable ordeal and so many more people were willing to travel regularly from their hometowns.
8. The automobile was a great labor and time-saving device, giving its owners more leisure time. Leisure pursuits, no longer solely for the very rich, became more important in developed countries.

9. Automobiles have been playing a vital part in the daily activities of our society.
10. With the improvement of people's living standard, some people have bought cars of their own, and others are planning to buy cars.
11. If conditions permit, owning a car can make us work more efficiently and life will become more convenient.
12. A car allows one to move freely.
13. With a car, there is no need to wait for the bus in the cold or under the burning sun.
14. Sitting in your own car is much more comfortable than having to wait a long time for the bus or train.
15. The automobile industry provides jobs for countless workers and strong support for other industries.

Disadvantages:

1. In the meantime, more often than not, the roads in big cities are jammed with cars and the air is filled with exhaust gas.
2. However, the fact cannot be ignored that cars are seriously polluting the air and filling the cities with unbearable noise, and even the fields in the countryside are disappearing, replaced by car parks and roads.
3. Cars have brought us joy and comfort, as well as injury and death.
4. What is more important, China, in which agriculture plays a leading role, will suffer a lot more than western countries if once stepping into the stage of popularization of cars.
5. So in my opinion, we should stop encouraging private cars, especially in big cities.
6. As a safer means of transport, buses ought to be given enough consideration and bicycle-riding should be encouraged.
7. It might be time for all of us to take much heed of the warnings of some experts to control the number of private cars in cities and to lay more emphasis on the environmental protection while enjoying the convenience provided by cars.
8. But automobiles have given rise to a series of problems.
9. More cars will result in more serious pollution.

Topic 8: Telephone or letter

Telephone:

1. One of the advantages of telephone communication is quite obvious: it can allow you

to begin instantly to communicate no matter how far you are away from each other. (4) As a result, fire alarm, robbery alarm and other emergency cases are often reported through telephone.

2. As a two-way communication, it also makes you clearly hear your friend's voice, and hence this communication will be easy and correct.
3. Communication is very important both in the past and at present and tends to be more essential in modern society. People nowadays can hardly imagine what communication looked like hundreds of years ago. It took several months for a mail from New York to San Francisco. With the development of transportation, letters can be sent much more quickly than ever before, but when the telephone appeared, most people have turned to it.
4. Communicating with other people by telephone is very convenient indeed, especially when you have something urgent. Let's suppose that you are a businessman in Beijing and are going to Hong Kong for a business meeting. When you get to the airport, someone tells you that the flight is cancelled because of the bad weather and you can not let the person who will meet you at the Hong Kong airport know the change by letter. What can you do? A telephone is the answer.
5. Today, with the quick rhythm of life people usually do not have as much time to write letters as before. Again telephone solves the problem.. Friends can chat through the electric line. It seems that telephone shortens the distance between people and men can keep in touch With each other more easily. From this point of view, telephone is one of the most wonderful inventions in the 20th century.
6. But the problem is that the cost for telephone calls is so high that many cannot afford it.
7. But sometimes it is not totally the case. People are becoming too dependent even when they do have time to write a letter, they prefer the telephone. With the little magical implement at hand, it is not difficult for a man to find excuse for not writing letters and feel at ease. Telephone is making people lazy. When a person writes, he must organize his mind to express his ideas and feelings more logically. People can not only greet each other but also exchange their thoughts by letters. At this point telephone lengthens the distance between people Progress turns to have more than one face.
8. The telephone has made the life in a modern city possible.
9. The telephone has almost killed the ancient art of letter writing, which used to be the only method of long distance communication.
10. Nowadays people begin to rely more and more heavily on the telephone to convey ideas and feelings to each other, because they feel it is more immediate and vivid when they hear the voice at the other end.

11. The past 20 years saw rapid development of telephone service in China.
12. Home phones which used to be thought of as luxury has become a common thing in more and more average homes.
13. The fast increase in home phones not only indicates that Chinese people are well-off, but also shows we are eager to participate in social communication and to acquire more and quicker information in different fields.
14. Telephones have been so popular that you won't be surprised to see so many people are making phone calls by their mobile phones while walking on streets or riding buses.
15. With the development of science and technology the telephone will serve people even better.
16. Every city has a closely-knit telephone network.
17. Mobile phones are much more convenient than the fixed phones.

Writing letter

1. By contrast, letter-writing is a formal way of communication: most of important notifications, such as those of acceptance, are made by letters.
2. Also, every letter communication has a record and can be kept for further reference when needed.
3. Yet, here again there is a disadvantage in it: it may take weeks for a letter to lead your information to a far destination.

Topic 9: 科技对环境的影响

1. An interesting fact about technology is that it can both hurt the environment and be our best hope for preventing or repairing such damage.
2. Techno1ogical progress is not the enemy of the environment but is perhaps its best friend, since it allows us to reduce humanity's footprint on the natural world.
3. High-tech agriculture boosts farm productivity, which means a cheaper food supply and more land spared for nature.
4. Better sewage treatment means that our rivers and stream can run free of pollutants.
5. Catalytic converters on the cars and better filters on power-plant smoke-stacks have greatly reduced smog, smoke and soot in the air.

Topic 10: 教学方式：严肃正规的 or 趣味性的

1. Attending lectures is very essential for students whose ability of independent learning is not fully established. Generally speaking, there are two different styles of lectures-the serious way and the entertaining way, which are adopted into classroom impartation. Although many of my peers are willing to choose the serious way, to my mind, I vote for the latter.
2. To be fair, the serious way of lecture allows us to acquire much information in class. But by this means students frequently fail to participate in class actively.
3. The teacher dominates the 50-minute period and the students are refrained from airing their opinions no matter whether they agree or disagree with what the teacher says.
4. Besides, students are expected to learn only what the teacher tells them, and have little chance to take advantage of others' ideas.
5. By contrast, the classroom lesson organized in an enjoyable, entertaining atmosphere usually offers students more than what they have expected.
6. A crack of joke may inspire students' interest and enthusiasm and then what they learn leaves on them an impression not easily forgotten.
7. In this kind of classes, in which heated debates are conducted, students often find out they are motivated by the pleasure of study.
8. It is quite obvious that, in an enjoyable classroom lesson, not only do we learn the knowledge in books but we also acquire some spiritual things brought about by the teacher's personality.
9. A light heart is always helpful.
10. Participation in the classroom is not only accepted but also expected of students in many courses.
11. Some professors base part of the final grade on the student's oral participation.
12. Although there are formal lectures during which the student has a passive role (i.e., listening and taking notes), many courses are organized around classroom discussions, student questions, and informal lectures.
13. In graduate seminars the professor has a "managerial" role and the students make presentations and lead discussions. The students do the actual teaching in these seminars.
14. A professor's teaching style is another factor that determines the degree and type of student participation. Some professors prefer to control discussion, while others

prefer to guide the class without dominating it. Many professors encourage students to question and challenge their ideas. Students who make assertions that contradict the professor's point of view should be prepared to substantiate their positions.

15. In the teaching of science and mathematics, the dominant mode of instruction is generally traditional, with teachers presenting formal lectures and students taking notes. However, new educational trends have emerged in the humanities and social sciences in the past two decades. Students in education, sociology, and psychology classes, for example, are often required to solve problems in groups, design projects, make presentations, and examine case studies.
16. Since some college or university courses are "applied" rather than theoretical, they stress "doing" and involvement.

Topic 11: 上学的目的

1. Education has become an essential part of one's life.
2. Now generally, from kindergarten to graduate school, it may run as long as 22 years.
3. Most children start school at the age of six.
4. They attend five or six years of elementary school and six years of high school (or secondary school).
5. After graduation from high school, a student can start his higher education in a two-year college, a four-year college, a university, or a specialized professional school.
6. Most colleges admit students on the basis of their Entrance Examination records.
7. Though great changes have taken place in China in the field of education, there is still a comparatively great part of the population of the country who cannot read and write.
8. There seems to be a growing tendency of life-long education for all.
9. The prosperity of a nation depends on the development of education.
10. Education, according to its stages, can be divided into preschool education, primary school education, middle school education, and higher education.
11. Better be unborn than untaught, for ignorance is the root of misfortune.
    —Plato, Ancient Greek philosopher
12. Education is the chief defense of nations.
13. Education begins its work with the first breath of the child.
14. Education is a progressive discovery of our ignorance.
15. Education has for its object the formation of character.

16. Only a nation of educated people could remain free.

—Thomas Jefferson, American president

17. he roots of education are bitter, but the fruit is sweet.

—Aristotle, Ancient Greek philosopher

18. The more we read, the more we are benefited.

19. Example is always more efficacious than precept.

20. The education of a man is never completed until he dies.

21. Knowledge is power. —Francis Bacon, British philosopher.

22. Activity is the only road to knowledge. —George Bernard Shaw, British dramatist.

23. A free man obtains knowledge from many sources besides books. —Thomas Jefferson, American president.

24. Experience is the father of wisdom and memory the mother.

—Charles Bernard, French philosopher.

25. Love is ever the beginning of knowledge as fire is of light.

26. Knowledge is a treasure, but practice is they key to it.

27. Knowledge advances by steps not by leaps.

28. Knowledge rests not only upon truth alone, but upon error also.

29. We would have new knowledge, we must get a whole world of new questions.

30. Knowledge makes humble; ignorance makes proud.

31. Thousands of children in our country are deprived of the opportunity to go to school by poverty.

32. Hope Project mainly depends on the contribution of urban people and overseas Chinese who care about the development of China's education.

33. Education can not only enrich people's knowledge, but also improve people's moral standard as a whole.

34. In the last two decades, owing to education, we witnessed a rapid development in industry, agriculture, science and technology in China.

35. It is the children's rights to receive education.

36. Helping a child go back to classroom will not cost one much, but will greatly benefit the society as well as the child.

37. It has been proved that the Hope Project is quite successful, and a lot of children have returned to school.

38. If the countryside is not developed, neither will be China.

39. It is quite necessary to set up the Hope Project, which aims that every citizen in our society lends a hand to the poor children who have no chance to go to school.

40. The economic development of our country and the status of China in the world depend mainly on the next generation.
41. Have you ever asked yourself why students go to school? You will probably say that they go to school to learn their own language and other languages, mathematics, history, science and all the other subjects. That is quite true. But why do the learn these?
42. We send our children to school to prepare them for the time when they will be big and will have to work for themselves.

Topic 12: 为什么上大学?

1. With the new higher education policies coming into effect, a growing number of college students, who are fully aware of the uncertainties of their future careers, are eager to know what they should learn in college. To wards the eagerness, students render quite different opinions.
2. As my high school years were drawing to a close, I turned over and over again in my mind the question of whether I should go to college. At times I did have some doubts. After careful consideration, however, I finally decided it was worthwhile to attend college.
3. Some of them hold that having a diploma is certainly the destination of the study in college. They believe that the diploma will guarantee favorable opportunities in the job-hunting campaigns. So their college lives are almost focused on the books which help them pursue decent scores in the exams. However, can a diploma be regarded as an equivalent for the success in the future? Under the marketing system, quite many college students tend to challenge this belief. They believe that it is most important to develop the personal interests and rewarding specialties in the college study. For this purpose, they of-ten have every reason to pride themselves on excellent academic achievements in the subjects they take a deep interest in, while they may flunk in other courses.
4. University as a significant cultural force has brought itself wide recognition and undeniable social appeal; therefore, studying in it is considered one of the most important and most valuable experiences in one's life and his academic performance in it will greatly affect his future. In our society, a degree, especially a higher one, usually means a decent and well-paid job, with the result that some people regard the degree as

the only thing valuable for college life. Admittedly, the degree is essential for graduates who expect a prosperous future, but it is by no means the only magical stepping-stone to success university grants us.

5. Firstly, because I was always hungry for knowledge and keen on learning, while in high school, I became more and more interested in such subjects as math, physics, and chemistry. I longed to explore much further into those areas.

6. As one of the modern college students, I firmly believe that college is a place where we learn how to learn. We should take best advantage of the chance to learn broadly-math, history, and various sciences, not merely for a diploma.

7. Secondly, because I knew a college education would provide me with opportunities for all-round development. I would play in musical groups, take part in sports, and join campus organizations. Involvement in various kinds of activities could help make me a well-rounded person.

8. Finally, I was aware that in today's world many professions require years of specialized training. Without a college education, it would be difficult for me to obtain a desirable position.

9. On the other hand, it is also quite necessary that we take a wide interest in computer, foreign languages or any other practical disciplines rather than just confine our-selves within textbooks so that we could show ourselves as versatile graduates in the future job-hunting.

10. What I can acquire during my stay in a university can be much more than a degree. In the first place, university provides me with an enjoyable atmosphere of study and of other activities. Associating with different people on campus, consulting with my instructors over a sensitive topic, and reading in the quiet library can strongly shape my inclination, mature my thoughts, widen my horizon, and enrich my personality, all of which serve as an all-round reward.

11. In the second, in college, I gain a sense of responsibility-one of the most important things I can get out of college. Nurtured in the atmosphere of college studies, I feel stronger responsibility for my motherland as well as for my family, and I grow more able to shoulder more social obligations.

12. In the third, experience tells us that it is not always absolutely true that the higher the degree, the better the job. Many great men, such as Einstein, made their startling contributions to human progress without a high degree or even without a good school record.

13. So as I see it, although a degree plays an important role in one's future career, it will

not determine the course of one's life. A university furnishes a student with a variety of valuables, among which the degree is important, but not the most important.

Topic 13: 读书和旅行

Reading

1. Do you know the most popular pastime in the world is reading? Now there are various kinds of books available and we can learn lots of things from them. Books become the main source of knowledge we obtain. There are about three advantages in dreading as follows.
2. First, books provide us with various aspects of knowledge. We can learn physics, chemistry, mathematics and philosophy etc, from books. These are all necessary for us. Without the scientific knowledge, a person will probably not know how to operate a washing machine and how to use a computer. Without all this knowledge, a person can not live a better life in the modern world.
3. Second, reading makes us understand the world more. We have one month and one thousand dollars. We can only travel to one or two places to learn how people live there. But how many books can we buy with the money and how many books can we finish in one month? All these books may contain information about dozens of places. We can learn more by reading than by traveling.
4. Third, reading is the most romantic and the safest kind of traveling. By reading, we can travel to the North Pole, without having to endure the freezing cold-we can also go the desert without having to fear the threat of thirst. We can also go back to the ancient times to have a look at the people's life without any difficulty.
5. But as students, we do not have enough time and money to travel around; and studying is the most important thing for us to do. So why not read as many books as possible when we are young? This way we can get enough knowledge, to serve the people and the society better. Anyway we will have enough chances to travel later.
6. The knowledge we gain from books and formal education enables us to learn about things that we have no opportunity to experience in daily life.
7. In this way, we won't repeat the mistakes of others and can build on their achievements.
8. Innovations do not come about through reading but through experimentation.
9. One can apply the skills and insights gained through the study of books to practical experience, making an already meaningful experience more meaningful.

10. Unless it is applied to real experiences, book knowledge remains theoretical and, in the end, is useless.

Traveling

1. Of course traveling gives us direct experiences. It is much more exciting and active than reading. It is necessary for a person to expand his horizon. When you have a chance or enough money and time, you can travel around the world. It will make your life more pleasant and make you have a deep understanding of the people and the world.
2. He who travels far knows much.
3. Travel, in the younger sort, is a part of education; in the older, a part of experience.
4. The world is a book, and those who do not travel read only a page.
5. With the general standard of living improving and the working week becoming shorter, more and more people are able to make a holiday trip to places of interest.
6. Travelling enriches your knowledge.
7. Travelling helps you to see new customs, eat new foods, and do new things.
8. Travelling also helps you to make new friends wherever you go, you are bound to meet with people.
9. The best means for getting knowledge of actual experience is travel.
10. However, travelling may cause some problems.

Topic 14: 大学生应不应该谈恋爱

1. According to a recent survey, roughly six out of every ten college graduates have the experience of dating with the opposite sex. The number is not a surprise at all, considering that the age of college students is usually between 18 and 24. What is really worth bothering to care for, however, is the serious problems love affairs have presented.
2. The alarming one is the increase in violent incidents owing to love on campus. When failing to win desirable affection from their lovers, some girl students tend to commit suicide while boys turn to knife and poison for revenge. Besides, it is a painful fact that boys obtain money needed for their love in an improper way. To please their girl friends, boy students always dress smartly, shop generously and eat out frequently; but when finding no other quicker way to make the money needed than by stealing

or cheating, they are on the way to imprisonment. Another sensitive problem is the growing pregnancy rate among girl students. The young students are subjected to blame for being too young to put themselves under sensible control, but school authorities cannot escape their share of responsibility.

3. Some college teachers argue that students should give up love for the sake of learning. They maintain that love is time-consuming and tears students away from learning, students' main task. If a student falls in love, he will certainly neglect his studies and cannot catch up with his class.

4. With regard to universities, they should offer more than practical lectures on education of love; for example, debates about love on campus should be regularly held among the students, thus making themselves clear about the rights and wrongs of their action. Also, they should appoint some special instructors whose job should center round psychology of students in love as well as those with troubles in love affairs. In short, schools should stop acting as onlookers dents, and perform full responsibilities as an institution of developing well-rounded talents.

5. Students, however, hold that forbidding love affairs among college students in not good. They take for example some of their friends who, falling in love, study harder and make greater progress in order to please their girl (or boy) friend. Some one else, on the contrary, who has not fallen in love, cannot concentrate on learning.

6. In my opinion, as a coin has two sides, love can be positive and negative. If you do not give yourself away in love but take it as a drive, you will make more progress in your learning and achieve much. But if you forget everything else except love, then you will become a "perfect" lover and a definite loser in your studies.

7. In love, those who are accustomed to self-centered ways of thinking learn to take care of others and be considerate of others.

8. Frequently going out on a date may result in frequent absence from classes, which will interfere with their studies.

Topic 15: 纯科学和应用科学

1. Pure science and applied science, as the two branches of science, are playing an increasingly important role in the development of a nation. They are mutually dependent and inter-acting in our practical life.

2. As the first productive force behind our social progress, science comprises two major branches. One is the pure science and the other is the applied science. The two branches play different roles in the societies in which we live.
3. Pure science is primarily concerned with the special methods of thought and action used in establishing relationships between the phenomena of the universe. These methods or theories or hypotheses, once verified or validated through practice and experiments, will become working principles of science. In carrying out this work, however, the pure scientist usually gives little thought to its application to practical affairs. Instead, he or she always confines all his or her attention to the interpretation of why and how events occur. Hence, in biochemistry, Watson and Crick's discovery of the molecular structure of DNA (Deoxyribo-Nucleic Acid) is said to be a typical example of pure science.
4. Pure science, which primarily deals with the development of theories establishing relationships between the phenomena of the universe, lays the ground for the development of applied science. Once sufficiently validated, these theories, including hypotheses and models, become the working laws or principles of science. Such theories will contribute greatly to the social progress if they are applied to practical affairs. But the problem is that the pure scientist usually confines his attention to explanations of how and why events occur and can not create instant material wealth, and that the pure scientific research, in the course of its own development, re-quires large amounts of money which our country cannot afford right now.
5. By contrast, applied science is directly related to the application of the working laws of pure science to the practical affairs of life. With the help of it, man can improve his ability to control his environment, thus leading to the invention of new techniques, processes and machines, etc. But a drawback lies in the fact that once deprived of the powerful backing of pure science, the development of applied science will be much limited and will remain at its existing levels.
6. Applied science, on the other hand, is directly concerned with the application of the working laws of pure science to our social life. This application directly results in the development of techniques, processes and machines, and then in the increase of man's control over his environment. Such activities as exploiting the findings of pure mathematics for the improvement of sampling procedures in agriculture or in other fields, developing the potentialities of atomic energy, and investigating the strength and uses of material, are all examples of the work of the applied scientist or technologist. Thus, it can be safely asserted that, with the advancement of human society, the

division between the pure scientist and the applied scientist will be more apparent.

7. From what has been discussed above, we may safely draw the conclusion that there is an inseparable relationship between the two branches. While advocating putting theoretical work into practice, we must encourage applied scientists or technologists to help develop our national industry, agriculture, transportation, communication, etc., and meanwhile not to ignore the further development of basic research. As long as we strike a proper balance between them, there will be a great leap in our science and technology.

Topic 16: 大学生，住校好，住在家里好？

1. Nowadays, there are two kinds of college students: day students and those who live on the campus. It is generally believed that both kinds of them will receive an equally good education. As a college student, however, I think the advantages of living on the campus always far outweigh those of staying at home.
2. Admittedly, the students living at home can feel the warmth of living because their parents help do everything for them, but they cannot get in to the real world of college. On the contrary, the students who live at college allow themselves to plunge into school activities, thus college becomes a world in itself in which they can be devoted totally to their studies.
3. Besides, students living at home do not have enough freedom. Like it or not, there are, from time to time, parents watching over them and telling them what to do, and so on. Those living in a dormitory at college, however, have more freedom and can build their own social maturity as they have to get along with many new, unknown people and this experience does help them grow.
4. Most importantly, if a student lives at home, he will be intellectually restricted because there are no discussions held with his peers at table and there is no access to the school library, either. By contrast, al-though living on campus is a bit hard for a person's material life, yet he enjoys the advantage of academic atmosphere without noise and some other distractions, and what is more, the library is just a stone's throw away.
5. So, as I see it, living on campus, as a precious opportunity for college students, is the best way of learning independence, and of understanding other people and society at large. Such an experience will definitely by of great benefit to him in his later career.

Topic 17: 为什么学英语?

1. Now, quite a number of English learners in China think as much of studying English as of seeking a better score in the exams like College English Tests (CET) Band IV and Band VI, and TOEFL. In class, meanwhile, many English teachers tend to expect students to be much concerned with passing these exams. Accordingly, the overrated exam value of English makes it quite necessary to repeatedly discuss the question of what we study English for.
2. There can be no doubt that English is one of the world's most widely used languages. People use a language in one of three ways: as a native language, as a second language, or as a foreign language. English is spoken as a native language by over three hundred million people in the United States, Britain, Australia, New Zealand, Canada, some caribbean countries and South Africa. As a second language, English is often necessary for official business, education, information and other activities in many countries, it is one of the few "working" languages of the United Nations.
3. It is said that English has become the language of international trade and transport. Most pilots in planes travelling from one country to another use it to talk with airports. All ships sailing on the oceans call for help by radio in it. It has been said that 60 percent of the world's radio broad casts and 70 percent of the world's mail uses English. At international sports meets, and international of scientists English is the language most commonly used and the most widely used.
4. English has in fact become the language of international cooperation is science and technology. The most advanced results in space, nuclear and computer research are published in it. A scientist who speaks and writes English is in closer touch with the scientists in other countries than one how doesn't
5. To many English learners, English is such a useful tool that they must focus their efforts on a proof of their English proficiency through exams. They believe that English may help them find a highly-paid job, get promoted or study abroad. On the other hand, in order to build up the students' power to pass the exams, many teachers often pay little attention to enlivening their lifeless classes. Obviously, what they don't seem to appreciate, no matter whether in English teaching or learning, is that English is a living language of communication. In fact, the emphasis on the exams that are seldom related to how to interact with native speakers hinders the use of English for communication. Under the pressure of exams, students have to center their learning around the

points that may be tested. As a result, many students who passed the Band VI fail to express face to face their ideas on jobs in English when interviewed by joint-venture companies.

6. Since the exams which may prove one's English proficiency will inevitably lead to the idea that the language is a tool for various certificates, I think that it is time now to adjust and broaden our English teaching. As English learners, we should be more motivated to use English for communication rather than see it merely as a "useful" tool".

Topic 18: 学校和家长都应对孩子负责任

1. Some people say parents should take the responsibility to conduct their children's behaviour, and tell them what is right or wrong, others say that it is the school's responsibility.
2. In my opinion, it is both the school's and the parents' responsibilities, for the parents are closer to their children than especially the mothers, who are the children's first teachers, can influence their children most. So the parents are playing a very important role in conducting their children what is wrong or right.
3. The school, which is the children's second teacher, is becoming more and more important. Some children may always consider their teacher's behaviour to be right and do exactly what the teacher instructs them do.
4. From this we can conclude that school and parents should both take the responsibility to conduct the children. Only in this way, can we make our children behave well in future. Obviously this is the best way we can take at present.

5. Our parents are our first and best teachers because they teach us the most important things in life, teach us continually and always have our best interests at heart.
6. Our parents begin teaching us the moment we are born, and what they teach us in those early years are the most important things we can learn. They teach us what is important in our own culture and how to get along with other people.
7. Our parents are always teaching us whether we realize it or not. They teach both in words and by example.
8. No teacher can take the place of our parents because they are our most devoted and best teachers.

Topic 19: 学生的兼职工作

1. Recent years, in the hope of earning both money and social experience, more and more students are inclined to take part-time jobs in their school time. As to whether it is worthwhile drawing much attention to the job from college study, people's attitudes vary greatly from person to person.
2. Some students think that taking up a part-time job may help themselves in many respects-stimulate learning more efficiently, explore the knowledge outside the books and even gain the financial independence.
3. And they hold the belief that the experience of taking the part-time job is a perfect preparation for their future job-hunting competition. "In order to meet the requirements of the job market", they often explain, "We have to gain enough confidence and modify our career orientation from our part-time jobs."
4. Yet there are still other students who show their objections to undertaking part-time jobs. They think that part-time jobs. They think that part-time jobs will have strong negative influence on study. And the work, which often makes a student under strong pressure and burden, can only be done at the cost of the time in which to join in various college activities. "I don't think such a thing is worth doing, " said one student who decided to quit his part-time job, "for even though I was earning money, it came at great cost. "
5. In my opinion, whether it is worthwhile taking a part-time job depends on our ability to deal with the relationship between study and work properly. There is no denying that part-time jobs are helpful to our sights and experiences. But if we only take it as a must for financial support, I think, we should put a top priority on whether it is a good help to our academic performance.
6. While it is true that a student's most important goal must be to learn and to do well at his studies, it does not need to be the only goal. In fact, a life which consists of only study is not balanced and may cause the student to miss out on other valuable learning experiences. In addition to bringing more balance to a student's life, part-time work can broaden his range of experience. He will have the opportunity to meet people from all walks of life and will be faced with a wider variety of problems to solve. Furthermore, work helps a student to develop greater independence, and earning his own pocket money can teach him how to handle his finances. Finally, a part-time job can help a student to develop a greater sense of responsibility, both for his own work and for that of the team he works with.

Topic 20: Spending money on artistic projects

For:

1. Enrich people's spiritual life, evoke people's feeling.
2. Part of the spiritual civilization construction.
3. Art is a revelation of social temper, which reveals the general state of mind of the majority.
4. Without arts, life would become dull and monotonous.
5. Provide more places of entertainment and recreation for citizens to enjoy their leisure time.
6. It is important to one's self-cultivation.
7. Improve one's intellect and sensitivity to beauty. Enlarge man's capacity for feelings, thoughts, and imaginations.
8. To boost local tourism. Most of these artistic projects are symbols of the city, which appeal to visitor from home and abroad.
9. Add beauty to the cityscape.
10. Upgrade the image and status of the city.
11. Give the residents a better living environment.
12. Improve the investment environment and attract investment as well.
13. Benefit future generations.
14. The improvement of a spiritual civilization boosts the material civilization.
15. It is a way of environment protection.
16. Create more job opportunities to release the unemployment situation.

Against:

1. High art appeals to only a small proportion of the population and thus benefits few.
2. We have a very limited budget. We should make full use of the taxpayers' money to benefit the common people.
3. China is still a developing country, which is short on funds. A thousand and one things remain to be taken care of.
4. There are still many people living below the poverty line, and many eligible children can not receive the basic education for lack of money.
5. Priority should without doubt be given to the development of infrastructure, not the building of art centers.

6. It is a waste of the government revenue.
7. It brings destruction to nature.

Topic 21: Should animals suffer for humans?

For:

1. Animals are our main food providers.
2. Animals are obedient and cheap helpers of human beings.
3. Animals are great entertainers for human beings.
4. Better that animals suffer than humans.
5. Tests are necessary to find cures to the diseases.
6. Realistic tests are necessary.
7. Hardly any advance in either human or veterinary medicine-cure, vaccine, operation, drug, and therapy-has come about without experiments on animals. For example, it may be impossible to get the data we need to determine the hazards of, say, radiation exposure or environmental pollutants without animal testing.

Against:

1. Not all animal tests are important.
2. Animals have rights too.
3. It is very cruel and barbaric to test on animals. It should be stopped on moral grounds alone.
4. It is very merciless to use animals in blood sports such as hunting, gunning or coursing.
5. Often computer simulation and tissue culture are possible and can achieve the similar results.
6. Modern technology has enabled us to produce some synthetic foods to replace animal meat.

第八章　范文

I 议论文

★ Topic 1:

Some people say college students should pay for all their tuition fees. Some people believe the government should pay for the tuition fees. What is your opinion?

Sample 1

In this time and age, higher education is advancing at an alarming rate. A sizable percentage of the people hold the opinion that the government should be responsible for the full tuition of college students. They claim that after graduation, college students will contribute much to the society. However, I am convinced that university students should pay for their tuition fees.

The main reason is that it can ensure the quality of college education. College education needs many well-paid professors and various advanced facilities. In other words, it needs a great sum of money. If the college students do not pay the tuition fee, it will lay a heavy burden on the government. If the government is unable to invest enough money on university education because of the limited budget, the quality of education cannot be ensured.

It might also be noted that it is quite fair to require students to pay the full tuition. It is unnecessary that all the citizens go to colleges. Some high school leavers give up their further study because they have their own life aim. That is to say, going to university is a totally personal choice. Therefore, it is not unreasonable that the people who make such choice pay for it.

Some people may say that students from the countryside and undeveloped areas cannot go to college if students are required to pay full tuition. In fact, there are some feasible methods to solve the problem. The first option is the bank loan, although it may have to be paid back at a later date. In addition, the students should be encouraged to study hard to win scholarship. Furthermore, they can work part-time to earn money to cover some expenses.

So, as I see it, college students should pay for the full tuition. It can guarantee the quality of higher education. It is a reasonable practice. What is more, students from poor families still can go to college even if they have to pay the full tuition.

Sample 2

In this time and age, higher education is advancing at an alarming rate. A sizable percentage of the people hold the opinion that the government should be responsible for the full tuition of college students. They claim that after graduation, college students will contribute much to the society. However, I am convinced that university students should pay for their tuition fees.

First of all, it can ensure the quality of college education. Compared with the elementary and secondary education, the college education is operating in a quite different system. It needs many well-paid professors and various advanced facilities. In other words, it needs a great sum of money. If the college students do not pay the tuition fee, it will lay heavy burden on the government. If the government is unable to invest enough money on university education because of the limited budget, the quality of education cannot be ensured.

In the second place, it is a quite fair practice. Most of the countries in the world are supporting the elementary and secondary education. It is reasonable since the citizens should be encouraged to receive basic education. However, it is unnecessary that all the citizens go to colleges. Some high school leavers give up their further study because they have their own life aim. That is to say, going to university is totally a personal choice. Therefore it is not unreasonable that the people who make such choice pay for it.

From the above views, I hold the opinion that college students should pay for the full tuition.

It can guarantee the quality of higher education. Moreover, it is a reasonable practice.

★ Topic 2:

What are the advantages and disadvantages of the Internet?

Sample 1

In recent years, the Internet has been gaining its popularity at an amazing rate. Some people suggest that the Internet brings us a lot of benefits. But on the other hand, there are also many people who strongly advocate that its drawbacks should not be ignored. It is quite understandable that people from different backgrounds put different interpretations on the same issue.

Those who believe that the Internet has many advantages give their reasons as follows. In the first place, the Internet brings us great convenience and efficiency. For example, we can send e-mails to our friends in other countries in a few minutes while sending a traditional letter takes us at least a week and costs much. In the second place, we can make friends with people from all parts of the world. It overcomes the geographical barriers and makes the world smaller. Furthermore, the Internet accelerates the flow of information and it spreads education to all corners of the globe. We can have easy and quick access to the latest information worldwide.

However, the other side of the coin voices its strong opposition, saying that the Internet has many weaknesses. For one thing, it can easily lead to psychological problems. A person who is addicted to the Internet tends to be isolated, self-centered and unsociable. For another, there is a sharp rise in the number of cyber crimes. More and more financial crimes such as money laundering are committed by the Internet. In addition, it has negative impacts on young people because there are a lot of obscene and violent contents on line. If children see a lot of violence, it makes them resort to brutal behaviors when arguments happen.

For my part, I completely agree with the latter view that the Internet has more disadvantages. It gives rise to people's mental problems. It results in various computer crimes. What is more, it is harmful to the growth of youngsters. Something should be done as soon as possible to protect people from the negative effects of the Internet.

Sample 2

In recent years, the Internet has been gaining its popularity at an amazing rate. It seems that anyone who knows little about the Internet is out of date and lags far behind the times. The Internet plays such an important role that it undeniably becomes the biggest concern of the world.

Those who favor that the Internet has many advantages give their reasons as follows. In the first place, the Internet brings us great convenience and efficiency. For example, we can send e-mails to our friends in other countries in a few minutes while sending a traditional letter takes us at least a week and costs much. In the second place, we can make friends with people from all parts of the world. It overcomes the geographical barriers and makes the world smaller. Furthermore, the Internet accelerates the flow of information and it spreads education to all corners of the globe. We can have easy and quick access to the latest information worldwide.

However, the other side of the coin voices its strong opposition, saying that the Internet has many weaknesses. For one thing, it can easily lead to psychological problems. A person who is addicted to the Internet tends to be isolated, self-centered and unsociable. For another, there is a sharp rise in the number of cyber crimes. More and more financial crimes such as money laundering are committed by the Internet. In addition, it has negative impacts on young people because there are a lot of obscene and violent contents on line. If children see a lot of violence, it makes them resort to brutal behaviors when arguments happen.

From my point of view, the Internet in itself is neither good nor bad. It makes us work more efficiently and plays an educational role in our daily life. At the same time, it gives rise to people's mental problems and results in various computer crimes. As the proverb says, fire is not only a good servant, but also a bad master. What we must do is to encourage the strengths and diminish the weaknesses as much as possible.

★ Topic 3:

Some people think that examinations have some bad effects on both students and teachers. Some people say they have good effects on education. What is your opinion?

Sample 1

From elementary school to university, students have to take many examinations. They may even regard examinations as an indispensable part of their life. In most schools and colleges, examinations are used as the chief means of deciding whether a student succeeds or fails in a subject. However, in my opinion, even if examinations do the job efficiently, they have many negative effects on students and teachers.

First of all, tests are unable to evaluate one's true ability. They can only test memory or the skill of working rapidly under pressure. In other words, it does not mean that all of those who get high scores on examinations possess creativity to deal with various problems. There are many stories of people who fail in their exams, but turn out to be great scientists or successful entrepreneurs.

Another effect is that examinations cultivate bad study habits. Students tend to lay too much emphasis on the content which will be tested. They are encouraged to memorize rather than to think. Moreover, examinations cause cramming before the exam. However after the examination, most students forget nearly all the information and facts they just put into their heads.

Finally, examinations lower the standards of teaching as well. They deprive teachers of all freedom. Since teachers themselves are often judged by examination results, they have to train students in test-taking techniques instead of teaching their subjects. Furthermore, students are required to learn only what teachers tell them.

In conclusion, although examinations have been used in the past, they exert adverse impacts on education. They cannot assess a student's performance in learning. They make students form bad study habits. In addition, teaching standards are reduced.

Sample 2

In the long history of human education, great changes have taken place in every field of study. However, testing a person by examinations is still regarded as the only reliable and feasible method to measure one's knowledge and ability. From elementary schools to universities, students have to take many examinations. They even regard examinations as an indispensable part of their life.

Some people hold that examinations have negative impacts on both students and teachers. First of all, tests are unable to evaluate one's true ability. They can only test memory or the skill of working rapidly under pressure. Secondly, examinations encourage bad study habits. Students tend to lay too much emphasis on the content that will be tested. They are encouraged to memorize rather than to think. Finally, examinations lower the standards of teaching. Teachers have to train students in test-taking techniques instead of teaching their subjects.

Many other people, however, believe examinations have some advantages. In the first place, they serve as a driving force to stimulate students to work hard. Laziness is part of human nature. Without the pressure of tests, students tend to ignore their studies. Moreover, the results of examinations function as mirrors for both students and teachers. Students can assess themselves and teachers can adjust their teaching method according to the information they obtain from examination. Finally, till now no better methods have been discovered to replace examinations. Other forms of assessment are too time-consuming and therefore are infeasible.

In my opinion, examinations have positive impacts on both students and teachers. They make students work hard. They also provide an objective standard by which the students can assess themselves and teachers can know what they should do next. Furthermore, at present no better methods are available. Therefore, I am sure examinations will continue to play an essential role in education.

★ Topic 4:

In recent years, many young people have decided to further their study abroad. What are the benefits and drawbacks of studying abroad?

Sample

People's living standards have improved over the years and many parents tend to pay more attention to their children's education. Therefore, more and more young people choose to go abroad to pursue their higher education. Frankly speaking, studying overseas has both its advantages and disadvantages.

Critics argue that there are many good reasons against further study abroad. For one thing, living far away from home, students will suffer from loneliness and homesickness. Overseas students often feel disoriented and depressed from lack of adequate knowledge and understanding of the local customs and lifestyle. For another, many students do not want to return to their native country after graduation because most of them want to seek a more comfortable life and a brighter future overseas. This may result in a serious brain-drain and our country will inevitably incur a huge loss of talents.

Proponents claim that overseas study has so many advantages. First of all, it can broaden the students' horizons. They get a chance to experience a totally different culture. The knowledge of high technology and social customs acquired in the other countries helps them to become more open-minded. Secondly, in terms of academic development, overseas study possesses several distinct advantages. Students can learn advanced science and technology. The book resources are more up-to-date. The professors are aware of all the latest development in their fields. Therefore the standard of teaching is much higher. Thirdly, when they finish their studies abroad, they will have more choices in their future careers. All the above merits are conducive to their self-betterment and self-realization.

In my opinion, while overseas study has its drawbacks, the advantages are obvious. It can broaden one's horizon. Students have easy access to the first-rate facilities and the latest development in science and technology. When they finish their study, students have more job opportunities. Therefore, as long as it is financially feasible, an overseas education may do a person more good than harm.

★ Topic 5:

When a student chooses the future career, what factors and whose opinions should he consider?

Sample

Choosing the right career is regarded as a turning point in one's life. It is so crucial that we can not afford to make a single mistake. However, it is always not easy to make a satisfying choice. Sometimes we find ourselves involved in dilemmas. How to decide upon the future career then? To my mind, the following factors need to be taken into consideration.

In the first place, make sure that you have an objective understanding of your ability as well as an interest so that you will know which occupation is suitable for you. Second, you should consider the prospect of the job. That is to say, is it a promising one which will offer you opportunities of promotion and self-betterment? Last but not least, your salary is undoubtedly an important element. There is no denying that to live a stable life requires a certain amount of money.

As the proverb goes, two heads are better than one. When you choose a job, always remember to talk with parents, teachers or anyone you trust. They possess rich experience and a life time of knowledge from which you are sure to benefit. They know you best and can offer you most sincere advice. Keep in mind the old saying that it is good to learn at another man's cost. Furthermore, you may also seek advice from the career advisory office they are always ready to provide professional suggestion.

In short, you should be sure that your choice is based on careful consideration from every angle. Also do not hesitate to seek advice from the people around you. In this way I am sure you are bound to obtain a desirable career in which your talents and intelligence can be fully displayed.

★ Topic 6:

In many countries children are engaged in some kind of paid work. Some people regard this as completely wrong, while others consider it as valuable work experience, important for learning and taking responsibility.
What are your opinions on this?

Sample

The issue of children doing paid work is a complex and sensitive one. It is difficult to say who has the right to judge whether children working is 'wrong' or 'valuable'. Opinions will also differ as to 'learning' benefits: no doubt teachers and factory owners, for example, would have varying concerns.

An important consideration is the kind of work undertaken. Young children doing arduous and repetitive tasks on a factory production line, for example, are less likely to be 'learning' than older children helping in an old people's home. There are health and safety issues to be considered as well. It is an unfortunate fact that many employers may prefer to use the services of children simply to save money by paying them less than adults and it is this type of exploitation that should be discouraged.

However, in many countries children work because their families need the additional income, no matter how small. This was certainly the case in the past in many industrialized countries, and it is very difficult to judge that it is wrong for children today to contribute to the family income in this way.

Nevertheless, in better economic circumstances, few parents would choose to send their children out to full-time paid work. If learning responsibilities and work experience are considered to be important, then children can acquire these by having light, part-time jobs or even doing tasks such as helping their parents around the family home, which are unpaid, buy undoubtedly of value in children's development.

★ Topic 7:

With the amazing development of computer science, computers can translate all kinds of languages well so our children don't need to learn more languages in the future. To what extent do you agree or disagree with this view?

Sample

With the amazing developments in computer science, and with the assistance of some great software, people can use computers to translate many kinds of language well. Therefore, some people think that our children won't need to learn more languages in the future. Despite the advantages advocated by these people, I am totally against this view.

It is known to all that with more international contacts and exchanges, foreign languages will become more and more important in the cross-cultural interaction. In opposition to the idea that the children won't need to learn more languages, there will be a greater tendency for them to know more than one foreign language so as to communicate with people from other countries on many occasions where computer translation can not play a part.

Another significant aspect is that language, as something indispensable to human beings, has existed almost as long as human beings. It represents a person's intellectual development, so does language learning. Most significant of all, although computers can be of great help to human beings, they can never replace human brains or surpass human intelligence. Take computer translation as an example, translation itself is an art rather than a branch of complete science. Mechanical translation sometimes is hardly understandable or readable without human revision. Machines can only translate literally, but fail to read between the lines, not to mention to appreciate the prime of the literary works. Some mechanical versions are very obscure and funny.

To my mind, language is a precious gift with which human beings are endowed with nature. No matter how advanced technology and science are, language will never vanish and be replaced. Instead it will become more essential and practical for children to master more than one language in the future, and so possess more competitive advantages over others in the future rat race.

★ Topic 8:

Nowadays, nurseries and kindergartens take care of children from an early age, so women can return to their jobs and children can get used to interacting with society early. Is this a good thing? What's your opinion?

Sample

With the social competition becoming keener and fiercer, a growing number of people have decided to send their children to nursery schools at an earlier age so that the mothers can be freed from child-care and pursue their own careers. Recently there had arisen a heated debate over whether it is wise to do so. People's views, however, are divergent on the matter in question.

People who advocate that children should be sent to nurseries earlier, have sound reasons.

Firstly, the period between 2 and 3 years old is crucial for a child's development in intelligence, character and social adaptability, so it is quite beneficial for them to receive systematic and scientific care as well as rudimentary knowledge from well-trained professionals. Secondly, in China, especially in cities, most children are the only child in the family. Therefore they need more opportunities to temper themselves and communicate with their peers. Meanwhile, it also helps them cultivate an independent spirit, and learn to cooperate and compromise. In a word, it will help children build a strong and well-rounded character. Last of all, sending children to nursery schools sooner enables mothers to pursue their careers, which will certainly increase the family's total income. This in turn ensures a better living condition for the children.

However, just as a coin has its two sides, sending children to nurseries at an early age also has two faces. Some people worry that it may lead to poorer parent-child relationship for lack of emotional communication, which will exert an irreparably negative impact on the psychological development of the children. As well all know, parents are the first teachers of their children. Moreover, there is also the possibility of lacking adequate care and attention because there are so many children in a class. Apart from these, there may be some potential dangers for the children who are too young to be able to take care of themselves. Lastly, some people also show concern over the nutrition and hygiene of the food provided by the nurseries. In short, they think the losses outweighs the gains.

Based on the reasons presented above, I think the pros outweigh the cons. By sending children to nurseries at an earlier age, mothers can enjoy the pleasure of working and bring more money back home. At the same time it is also conducive to the overall growth of the children involved.

★ Topic 9:

Corporal punishment has been practiced in many schools for quite a long time. In recent years, people's attitudes towards this practice have undergone drastic changes. Nowadays many people strongly oppose it. Should corporal punishment be abolished?

Sample

Cases of corporal punishment are reported to have taken place in schools now and then. The issue of whether it is good or not to exercise such physical punishment has aroused a heated discussions all over the country.

Those who have already benefited from practicing it sing high praise of it. They claim that some children are just too naughty to be taught. The claim that if these children are unaware of this punishment, they just don't know what discipline means. Through corporal punishment, these difficult children learn to obey school rules and discover how to they should behave themselves. Eventually, they will become well-disciplined and good-mannered students.

But there are also people who are strongly opposed to this kind of punishment. They contend that corporal punishment should be forbidden in schools. There are several reasons for this. Firstly, this is indeed a very uncivilized form of teaching. Schools are places where students receive formal education and learn to behave well. If teachers exercise corporal punishment on the so-called "bad" students, other students may follow suit. Just as the old saying goes: "violence begets violence.", they may learn to resort to violence and become rebellious against teachers and even against society. Secondly, great harm may be done to the student's body. There are already many such cases in the news this year, in one, a student lost their hearing because of his teacher's cruelty. Thirdly, students may be hurt psychologically. Some students are naughty, but they are not really bad students who are unteachable. They are eager to learn well too. If teachers are so rude and violent to them, they can be emotionally damaged and may become hostile to people and things around them. This is detrimental to the students' overall development. Fourthly, children's rights are violated. Children are human beings too. They enjoy the same equal rights as we adults do. Teachers have no right to exercise corporal punishment on them. Obviously, this kind of education is both undesirable and pernicious.

When considering the reasoning of both sides, I am inclined to take sides with the latter. Corporal punishment should by all means be forbidden in schools. We teachers are engineers of the soul. Therefore we should always love our students, be patient to them and try our best to facilitate them to develop in a correct direction.

★ Topic 10:

Advertisements are getting their way into people's lives. Discuss the effects of advertisements on people. Should all ads be banned?

Sample

Everywhere, and almost at any time, we find ourselves surrounded by all kinds of advertisements, advertisements on TV, in newspapers, on buses, on streets, and even on a small ball-point pen. We may safely declare that we live in a world of advertisements.

Manufacturers try every means to propagate their commodities. This world is flooded with many questionable advertisements, which are boldly exaggerated, mislead and fly in the face of truth. Naturally, consumers are the victims and manufacturers the beneficiaries. The abuse of advertising also gives rise to unhealthy competition among manufacturers. In view of these, some people have proposed to impose restrictions on advertising or even to ban it. Some people even consider their rights to be infringed upon by the pages of ads they find stuffed into their mailboxes and into their hands.

It is true that the abuse and hypocrisy of advertisements are really irritating, but there also exist some benefits in advertising. For one thing, advertising, as a means of sales promotion, helps consumers to select goods. People can judge for themselves what to buy. For another, advertisements have become beautiful ornaments to our lives, making our life colorful with beautiful, artistic pictures and words. Advertising is an art, similar to other artistic forms. Good advertisements enrich life and edify people.

I agree that there should be some restrictions on advertising, but they should not be banned. We can take some measures to wipe out the untruthful practices in making ads. For example, there are laws and rules for advertising. What we must make sure is that the false ads are eliminated and the true is retained. In this way, advertising may serve people better.

★ Topic 11:

Along with the amazing development of society, more and more people have begun to realize that only peace can ensure human prosperity. In recent years, some people have proposed that compulsory military service should be abolished. Do you agree or not? Give your reasons.

Sample

In many countries, children are called upon for military service when they are 18 years old nowadays. Meanwhile, in China, especially in lots of universities, freshmen are required to take military training before they begin to study. It seems that it is a must in the growth-process of the young. However, is it proper to maintain military service in an era characterized by peace and development? This question is a very controversial one. In my opinion, as the proverb goes:"Every coin has its two sides", military service, is no exception.

We can't deny that we have benefited a lot from military service. Firstly, it offers a good way to strengthen a person not only physically but also psychologically. When one is enlisted, he must act as an army man. No matter how tired he becomes during the difficult training, he must clench his teeth and carry on. Gradually, a strong character can be built up. And he epitomizes the virtues of perseverance and fidelity. Secondly, military training arouses people's awareness of discipline and unity. In the army, everything is fixed. One must obey the rules and do what he is scheduled to do promptly. Also, teamwork spirit and unity are very important for soldiers if they want to achieve a task perfectly. Thirdly, every citizen has the obligation to strengthen national defense, not just the young in the army. Once they join the army, they shoulder the responsibility of maintaining the stability and unity of their country. This helps to form a strong sense of patriotism, which all countries should foster.

Despite the advantages the military service has, it has some very serious disadvantages. In the army, no one is allowed to say "no" to an order. Such a discipline may possibly lead to bullying and conformity. "Yes Boys" and "Yes Girls" are found everywhere. Their lack of creativity and individuality will eventually turn into lack of vitality of their nation. What's more, it is a step away from peace. If it goes to extremeness, military service will inflict a fear called "MILITARISM" on us. People become militant. The threat of war will lead people all around the world into jeopardy.

All these opinions make sense, and it is consequently hard to decide which one is more reasonable. In my opinion, we'd better popularize the military service properly and restrain its bad effects. We should make it a good way to maintain peace and create a better world for us to live in.

II 学术类 (Academic) 图表作文

(一) 常用句型

1. 上升或下降

A. There was/were a/an

increase	grow	ascent	rise	surge
decrease	decline	reduce	fall	drop

in the number of 描述对象, from 起始时间 at about 起始数据 to 终点时间 at about 终点数据.

B. The number of 描述对象

increased	ascended	grew	rose	surged
decreased	declined	reduced	fell	dropped

greatly	sharply	rapidly	significantly	dramatically
slowly	slightly	little	moderately	modestly

from 起始时间 at about 起始数据 to 终点时间 at about 终点数据.

2. 稳定或波动

There was/were a fluctuation/fluctuations in the trend of 描述对象, from TIME-1 to TIME-1 and from TIME-2 to TIME-2.

The trend of 描述对象 remained stable/ stayed still/ kept the level for about 一段 TIME(起点 to 终点) at about 数据.

3. 最高点或最低点

At/In/On 时间, the number of 描述对象 reached its

highest point	peak	summit	top
lowest point	bottom	dead line	

at about 数据, then it began to decrease/ increase.

4. 平均数和总结

As a whole/ To sum up/ In a conclusion, throughout 整个时间(横轴), the average number of 曲线A was larger/ smaller than that of 曲线B (NUM & NUM).

5. 比较句型

Compared with 柱形A, the number of 柱形B was 数据(差值) larger/smaller in/at 范围.

In/At 范围, the number of 柱形A was 数据(差值) larger/smaller than that of 柱形B.

6. 发展趋势相似或相同

The trend of 柱形A was similar as 柱形B.

The trend of 柱形A and 柱形B were the same.

The trend of 柱形A and 柱形B had little difference.

7. 占最大或最小

描述对象 took up the largest percentage of 范围, 数据(**%).

描述对象 was taking up the smallest percentage of 范围, 数据 (**%).

描述对象 was the largest section of 范围, 数据 (**%).

8. 第二,三大或是小

After that, 描述对象 was the second largest part of 范围, 数据(**%).

Next to it, there was 描述对象 which took up 数据 (**%).

9. 居中的

Between/Among them, *** and *** took up 数据 (**%) and 数据 (**%) respectively/separately.

The rest of 范围 were medium, *** and *** were about 数据 (**%) and 数据 (**%).

10. 相比较(求差)

The amount of *** was 数据(差值) larger/smaller than that of ***.

Compared with ***, the number of *** was larger/smaller(数据 & 数据).

11. 相结合(求和)

The total amount of *** and *** was 数据 (**%)

Coincidentally, the total number of *** and *** was 数据 (**%).

12. 倍数和分数

分数是由基数词和序数词一起来表示的。基数词作分子，序数词作分母，除了分子是“1”以外，其它情况下序数词都要用复数形式。

The number of 描述对象-A was 分数 of 描述对象-B.

描述对象-A was 分数 of the number of 描述对象-B.

The number of 描述对象-A was 基数词 times 形容词(比较级) than that of 描述对象-B.

（二）范文

You should spend about 20 minutes on this task.

The chart below shows the amount of leisure time enjoyed by men and women of different employment status.

Write a report for a university lecturer describing the information shown below.

Write at least 150 words.

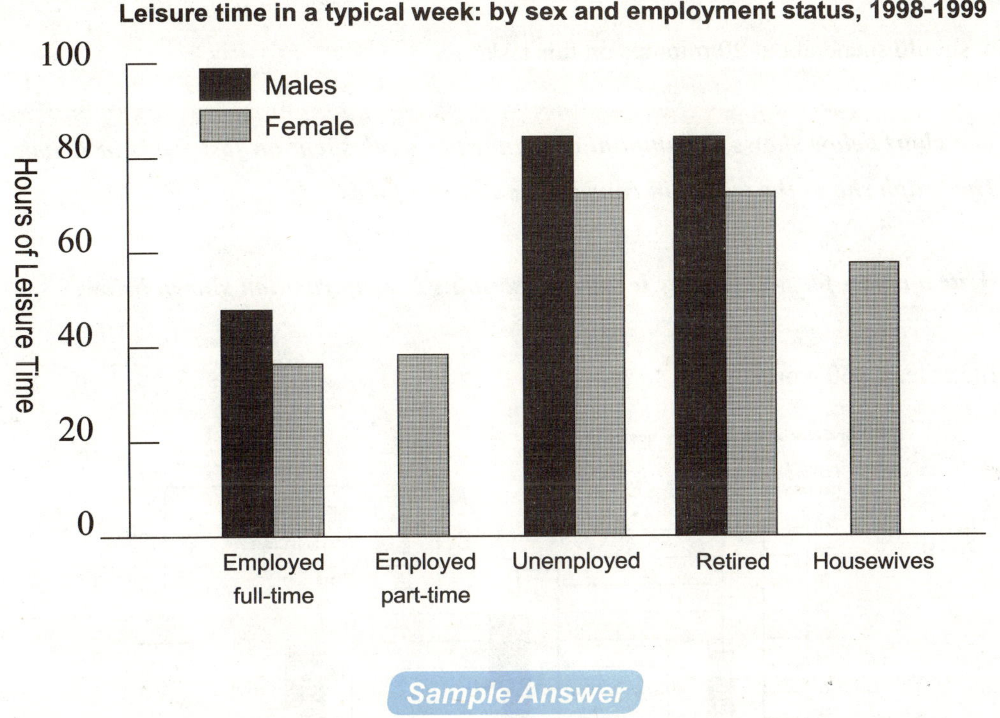

Sample Answer

The chart shows the number of hours of leisure enjoyed by men and women in a typical week in 1998-1999, according to gender and employment status.

Among those employed full-time, men on average had fifty hours of leisure, whereas women had approximately thirty-seven hours. There were no figures given for male part-time workers, but female part-timers had forty hours of leisure time, only slightly more than women in full-time employment, perhaps reflecting their work in the home.

In the unemployed and retired categories, leisure time showed an increase for both sexes, as might have been expected. Here too, men enjoyed more leisure time-over eighty hours, compared with seventy hours for women, perhaps once again reflecting the fact that women spend more time working in the home than men.

Lastly, housewives enjoyed approximately fifty-four hours of leisure, on average. There were no figures given for househusbands! Overall, the chart demonstrates that in the categories for which statistics on male leisure time were available, men enjoyed at least ten hours of extra leisure time.

You should spend about 20 minutes on this task.

> ***The chart below shows the amount of money per week spent on fast foods in Britain. The graph shows the trends in consumption of fast foods.***
>
> ***Write a report for a university lecturer describing the information shown below.***

Write at least 150 words.

Expenditure on fast foods by income groups

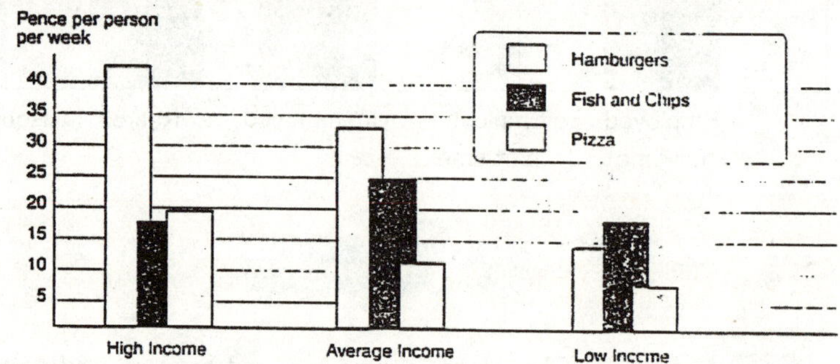

Consumption of fast foods 1970 - 1990

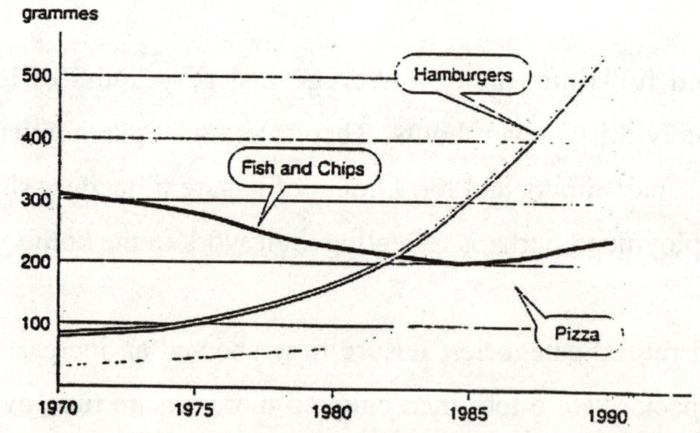

Sample Answer

The bar chart shows the amount of money expended on fast food according to three different income groups. Hamburger is the most popular fast food in the high and average income groups. People in high income spend over 40 pence per person per weak on the consumption of hamburger. Although fish and chips is the most popular food for those in low income, it is the least popular for those in the high income. Pizza, on the other hand, is not very popular among the low-income group.

The line graph indicates the general pattern of fast food consumption between 1970 and 1990. Obviously, there was a sharp increase in the consumption of hamburger during this time period. In 1970, people in Britain ate less than 100 grammes of hamburger per person per week. By 1990, this number increased to over 500 grammes. Pizza also increased but it was not so dramatic. Fish and chips, however, dropped slightly. Before around 1983, Fish and chips was the most popular fast food. However, after that, hamburger increased sharply and it became much more popular than the other two fast foods.

You should spend about 20 minutes on this task.

Many women want or need to continue working even after they have children. The charts below show the working patterns of mothers with young children to care for.

Write a report for a university lecturer describing the information in the charts below.

Write at least 150 words.

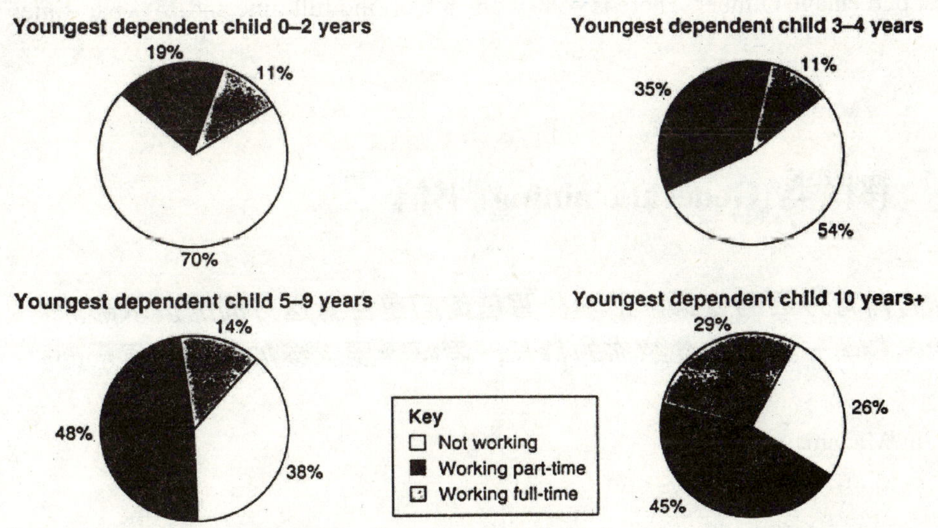

Here is how a student might have answered this task.

Sample Answer

In Great Britain, there are many women who want or need to continue working even after they have children. The four charts show the working patterns of mothers with young children to care for.

At first, mothers with their youngest dependent child aged 0~2 years, there is 11% women working full-time and 19% women working part time. The women who are not working is 70%.

The mothers with youngest dependent child aged between 3 to 4 years, almost half of them not work. There are 46% women working part time and the women who are working full time is 11%. It increases.

Then, the mothers with youngest dependent child aged between 5~9 years 38% of them are not working. There is 48% women working part time and the women who are working full time is 14%. The number of women working full time was increase in this chart and the number of working part time increase 18% from chart 2 and increase 29% from chart 1.

Finally, the chart 4 showed that the mother with dependent child aged 10 years has the biggest percentage number. There is 45% women working full time and 25% part time.

III 移民类 (General training) 书信

1. 你有体育方面的专长，给学校写信询问是否有这方面的俱乐部。给学校写一封信，介绍你的特长，爱好，要求参加学校的俱乐部。

Dear Sir /Madam,

I'm writing to ask if there is a tennis club in your university.

I'm planning to study in your university this summer for 2 years. I have specialty in playing tennis. I began exercise in tennis training and playing when I was 10 years old. The best result I have gained for the sport is that I won the championship in Peking University in 1998. When I go to your university, I hope there is a tennis club where I can improve my tennis skills, learn more knowledge from coaches, have partners who can play with me and participate in all kinds of related activities. In this way, my study life would be interesting. I was wondering if there is such a tennis club in your university and how I could join it.

I'm looking forward to your reply. Your kind help would be greatly appreciated.

Yours sincerely,
Fan Wang

2. 组织去剑桥大学参观，给对方写一封信，租用对方的图书馆。

Dear Sir /Madam,

I'm writing to ask if I could rent the library of your university on June 5th.

Cambridge is one of the most famous universities in Britain, which attracts many high school graduates. Our school is planning to organize some students to visit your university on June 5th so that they can know it better. In the morning, they will visit your beautiful campus. In the afternoon, I'll invite two professors to introduce the history of your university, teaching methods and teaching facilities to the students. There are about 40 students totally so I hope to rent a room in your library to hold the introduction meeting. I was wondering if I could rent it, how much I should pay for it and how I could rent it.

I'm looking forward to your reply. Your kind help would be greatly appreciated.

Yours sincerely,
Fan Wang

3. 给学校写信，自己对历史学科感兴趣，但认为计算机好找工作，希望学校给一些建议。

Dear Sir /Madam,

I am a student from Beijing No. 4 High School. I am planning to study in your university this summer. But which department should I take, history or computer science? I hope to get some advice from you.

I have shown great interest in history since my childhood. When I was a child, I was attracted by heroes of historical novels and was dreaming to be such kind of person. When I grew up, I felt deeply that history can make people wise and we can know the future from history. When I encountered a problem in my daily life and studying, I always could always find its answer from the history books. But it is said that graduate from computer department is easier to find a job and it usually is well-paid. Some young computer engineers have owned their house and private cars can prove this.

Do you think it is worthwhile for me to give up my interest to study a discipline which I don't like at all?

I'm looking forward to your reply. Your kind help would be greatly appreciated.

Yours sincerely,
Wang Fan

4. 求职信

Dear Sir /Madam,

From your advertisement on New York Times, May 5, I have learned that you need a programmer in your application department. I would be interested in exploring the possibility of obtaining such a position within your firm.

I received a Bachelor of Science degree in computer science from Beijing University in

June 1997. Since then I have been working in the Great IT Company as a programmer for 2 years and I have participated in several important projects. I am confident that I am an excellent C/C++ programmer whom you need. And I also have some experiences on database administration. Details of my educational background and working experience are contained in the enclosed resume.

May I have an appointment for an interview with you to discuss my qualifications in detail?

I'm looking forward to your reply. Thanks a lot.

Yours Sincerely,
Wang Fan

5. You traveled by plane last week and your suitcase was lost. You have still heard nothing from the airline company. Write to the airline and explain what happened. Describe your suitcase and tell them what was in it. Find out what they are going to do about it.
You should write at least 150 words.

You do NOT need to write your own address.
Begin your letter as follows:
Dear *********,

The following is a candidate's model answer:

Dear Sir,
I was one of the passengers who took the flight from Narita (Tokyo) to Heathrow (London) on 5 August. Unfortunately, my suitcase did not come out after the flight. Although I have explained this to Mr. McDonald who was in charge at the Luggage Claim Office, I have not heard from him as of now.

My suitcase is a grey Samsonite whose size is 70cm × 95cm. There are 3 stickers on one side and I heart shaped sticker on the other side. My initials "AR" are also written on both sides.

There are a few books and a copy of my thesis in that suitcase, which I need for the conference on 19 August.

So, I would deeply appreciate it if you could give me a prompt reply at your earliest convenient. My flight number, luggage claim number and address are written below.

Flight No: NH201
Luggage Claim No: 00026
Address: 64 Silver Street
London. NW165AL

Yours Faithfully,
Wang Fan

6. There is a mistake from the bill (单据) mailed by a bank, ask for correcting

Dear Sir /Madam,

I'm sorry to trouble you but I'm afraid I have to make a serious complaint about the bill mailed by your bank.

When I got the bill, I was surprised that it was much higher than usual. As usual, I spent about $500 per month. But the bill showed that I spent $5000 last month. I can promise that I did nothing special last month. How could I spend so much money?

After examining the bill, I realized that there must be something wrong with your billing system. I've never been to France, but there was a round trip to France airline ticket's cost in the bill. I can promise that I've never lent my credit card to anyone.

Please check the bill and give my money back. Otherwise, I will change to another bank.

Yours Sincerely,
Wang Fan

7. You are a student living in a university accommodation. The heating has not worked for some time. Write a letter to the management to complain.

Dear Sir,

I live in Room 201 in the first dormitory building. I am writing to express my dissatisfaction with the heating system.

When I got your brochure I was very glad and thought that I had found a nice accommodation. However, when I moved in, I found everything was so different from what the brochure told me. Beyond my tolerance is the heating system, because it has not worked till now. I have told the janitor about this, but have not got any feedback. It is getting colder and colder, so it has become very urgent. I hope you will send someone to repair it as soon as possible.

I would be very grateful if you kindly consider my request and maintain the heating system at once. I am looking forward to the day when it starts to work.

Or, I would like to move into a different room.

Yours sincerely,

Wang Fan

8. You are a tenant and have unintentionally damaged something that is the property of the landlord . Write to the landlord to describe how it happened and apologize.

Dear Mr. Johnson ,

I am writing to express my apology for having damaged the television in my room and I would like you to know that I am prepared to pay for the repair or for purchasing a similar one.

I was watching TV yesterday evening, with a cup of coffee in my hand. Then I heard the telephone ringing. I put the coffee on the top of the TV and went to the sitting room to answer the phone . It was a friend who asked me to go to a movie. We talked for some time and then I returned to my room . I had totally forgotten the coffee that I left on the top of TV. When I was putting on my coat , somehow I swept the cup over and the coffee spilt , some of which went inside of the TV and caused damage .

The TV is not working and I think it needs repairs from professional people. I would like to know what I should do.

Yours sincerely,

Wang Fan

9. You are travelling and have lost something that is expensive . The lost item is insured . Write to the insurance company to describe how it happened and ask for compensation .

Dear Sir or Madam,

I am one of your customers, and I just lost an expensive video recorder on a trip .

I joined in a holiday tour last week. But on March 12th, when I finished one day's sightseeing and went back to the hotel, I found my video recorder which was in a drawer missing. I had to recharge the batteries of the recorder so I did not bring it with me on that day. I asked the floor waiter about the recorder but he said he did not even notice it. I also complained to the manager of the hotel. He said he was sorry for my loss but he could do noting about it. So I had to call the police. When I returned from the trip , I remembered that some of my properties , including the recorder , were insured by your company . Therefore , I am writing to let you know that I would like to claim compensation from you .

I have enclosed a copy of the police statement .

I look forward to your timely reply .

Yours sincerely,

Wang Fan

第九章 写作素材

I 议论文

1. Topic: Love and Learning

许多大学教师主张禁止学生恋爱

大学生认为禁止无益，你的观点

Some college teachers argue that students should give up love for the sake of learning. They maintain that love is time-consuming and tears students away from learning, students' main task. If a student falls in love, he will certainly neglect his studies and cannot catch up with his class.

Students, however, hold that forbidding love affairs among college students is not good. They take for example some of their friends having fallen in love, study harder and make greater progress in order to please their girl (or boy) friends. Someone else, on the contrary, who has not fallen in love, cannot concentrate on learning.

In my opinion, as a coin has two sides, love can be both positive and negative. If you do not give yourself away in love but take it as a motivation, you will make more progress in your learning and achieve much. But if you forget everything else except love, then you will become a "perfect" lover and a definite loser in your studies.

2. Topic: Which One Do You Like: a Small Family or a Large Family?

大家庭的优点：成员之间可以互助　缺点：经常争吵

小家庭的优点：成员自由　缺点：比较忙碌

你的观点：小家庭

In ancient times the Chinese farmed for a living, always lived on the land inherited from their ancestors and never moved without important reasons. So they formed large families. But with the change of social structure and the increasing strength of individual independence, the number of small families is growing larger.

A large family may include three generations. Its benefit is that people can help each other in time of need. Unable to earn a living themselves, the grandparents in this family can be provided for by their sons or daughters. The third generation may be cared for by the grandparents. Thus the second generation can be absorbed in work without causing trouble at home. However, many people living together is sure to produce some conflict. Everybody's business is nobody's business. In other words, there is almost no privacy.

The good and bad sides of a small family are just the opposite of a large family. A member of a small family can freely express his (or her) feeling to his wife (or her husband) and children. The people of a small family do not have to do what they do not like under the mask of happiness. Of course, a young couple are busier than those of a large family in taking care of children. Asked whether I like a large family or a small family, I would answer: I like the latter. But I must emphasize one thing. It is important to keep frequent touch with your relatives if you live in a small family, and especially to support your parents when they are too old.

3. Topic: World Governments Should Conduct Serious Campaigns against Smoking.

吸烟有害健康，但政府不彻底禁烟，因税高
不禁烟的弊端：需治病，丧失生命
结论：应彻底禁烟

It is well known that there is a definite link between smoking and bronchial troubles, heart diseases and lung cancer. But, ignoring the danger, the governments of most countries have not stood for complete prohibition of cigarette smoking. Although a few governments have taken limited measures, the population continues to puff its way to a cancerous death.

You do not have to look very far to find out why the official reactions to medical findings have not been enthusiastic. The answer is simply money. As a wonderful commodity to tax, tobacco means billions of dollars to governments. Therefore, while pointing out that smoking may be harmful, the authorities do not shout too loudly about it.

Surely, this is a most short-sighted policy. While taxes is collected in vast sum, much larger amounts are spent on cancer research and on efforts to cure patients, not to mention countless valuable lives lost as victims of smoking. In the long run, it is high time that world governments conducted serious campaigns against smoking.

4. Topic: *Some people think that family is the most important influence on young adults. Other people think that friends are the most important influence on young adults. Which do you think is the most important influence? Give specific reasons for your answer.*

The process of growing up is very complex for every person. Among the countless factors which influence a person's growth, there are two conspicuous aspects: family and friends. After one is born, the first and nearest surroundings is the family in which he will grow up. So family does play a significant role in shaping a child's inclination and character. While, on the other hand, almost as soon as a child becomes old enough to communicate with other children, he begins having friends who sometimes influence him more rapidly than his family does. As far as I am concerned both influences are indispensable for a child's growth.

Several centuries ago, there was a world-famous family in Europe. More than 20 great scientists and mathematicians were received in this family, so there are so many formulas and laws with the name: Bernoulli. It is a forceful example of the influence of family. Because family are children's most direct source of knowledge and other experiences, those who are brought up in good family tend to possess many pleasant characters, and vice versa.

If we say that families offer the living environment, friends take another important part in shaping the child. They are connections between the child and the society. By associating with friends, one can gradually be introduced to society and become sociable. man is social creature so children should understand society, get used to it, and get pleasure out of it. To this point, friends greatly help. As for me, I have lots of friends who have many different opinions and personalities. Discussing the world with them enriches my thoughts, and playing with them builds up my personality. Frankly, I get a lot of valuable things from my friends.

Families offer us warmth and care. Friends give us strength and broaden our horizons. They both help us understand the world as it is. Both of them are the dearest parts in our life.

5. Topic: *Inventions such as eyeglasses and sewing machine have had an important effect on our lives. Choose another invention that you think is important. Give specific reasons for your choice.*

I ride a bicycle to get to work every day and have first hand experience of how the bicycle is very convenient in our daily lives. Beijing is called a city of bicycles. There are various kinds of bicycles from small to big ones ridden on all sorts of streets. My director, Professor Li, began to learn how to ride a bicycle last year, when she was fifty-three years old, and now she can ride her small bike to and from the laboratory every day.

The bicycle makes us easily go anywhere nearby. In China, there are not many private cars since an ordinary family cannot afford it. Bicycles can save time and make the owners move more quickly when traffic occurs during rush hours or any other troublesome periods.

Usually, riding a bicycle is favorable to a person's health. In modern times, life is very busy and time always seems limited. Using the time you spend in riding a bike to train your body is also a good way to follow.

In the beautiful seasons of spring and autumn, riding a bicycle to travel and appreciate the scenery is a wonderful experience. We can see buds on the tree branches, flowers in bloom, blue sky with white cloud and so on. With the breeze kissing our faces, it is a feeling beyond description.

Compared with cars, a bicycle has no environment problems. It is harmless to the air and people's health. It also saves energy and parking places, and it has less possibility of traffic jam than driving a car. Bicycle has been important in human life ever since the period after it was invented. I believe it will still be very necessary in the future.

6. Topic: *Some people think that parents should plan their children's leisure time carefully. Other people believe that children should decide for themselves how to spend their free time. Which idea do you agree with? Give reasons for your choice.*

As I remember, my parents were very strict with me during my childhood. No matter how I pleaded or tricked them to allow me to go out and play, the answer was invariably cruel: "Finish your homework first!" Moreover, my leisure time was arbitrarily divided into several parts: reading, writing, listening to the music, sporting, taking trips with my family, and so on. In those activities, my parents were my guides, partners, or competitors. But in my eyes, they were austere supervisors who gave me too little freedom. Sometimes I got very unhappy, crying and kicking the door close and open in a loud noise. But it was no use. In such an environment, I finished elementary school, junior high school and high school and became a university student.

Nowadays, when someone praises me for my academic excellence, I thank my parents, since it is they who taught me good study habits, though I was unaware. When I succeed in an experiment after many failures, I owe it to my parents who have encouraged me to "try, and try again" since the time I could remember. Not until today do I really understand their patience, their consideration and their deep love for me. What they gave me is not only the life of my body, but the life of my mind as well.

Little children are like young trees. In order to grow well, they need to be carefully irrigated, fertilized and trimmed. The question is not whether the parents should plan their children's leisure time carefully, but whether they can do that properly. Some parents control their children tightly but poorly. They do not understand them, and always expose adult standards on the young. Some parents indulge their child too much. They give him what he wants, and forgive him when he has done something wrong. They prepare everything for the child except the most important characteristic independence.

It is not an easy thing for parents to shape their children into a good person. But I think, with love and understanding, nothing is too hard.

7. Topic: *Many important natural resources such as water, forests, oil, etc. are running out in the world today. What should we do to protect them? Give specific examples to support your idea about one kind of these resources.*

I was born and grew up in a small village in the south which was surrounded by green mountains. During my lonely childhood, I often strolled in the mountains, picking up unknown flowers and fruits, and playing with little, pretty, shy animals. The mountains were covered with various grasses, bushes and trees. These were great treasures for me. I always had a good time in the mountains.

After I graduated from high school, I went to a big city in the north to enter a university. The life and environment there were quite different from that in my hometown. You could not see a single mountain in the city, nor could you even find a real hill. All around were grey buildings. What a dull picture! Although there were colorful light at the night, I often dreamed of my green mountains. Deep in my heart, they were my real home.

Several years later, I had the opportunity to go back home. How exciting I was when I approached my village. However, when I got off the train, I was shocked. Miserably I saw that my green mountains had disappeared. Hundreds of new buildings stood where green forests once existed. I was hurt.

Gone with my green hometown.

Gone with my pleasure in refreshing my heart in the green forests.

I know I am not the only one who has the miserable experience of losing his green hometown. We see and hear from newspaper, radio and TV programs that forests have been disappearing at an alarming rate in many places in the world. And we know that forests are essential for many aspects of human life. They provide wood, food, mild climate and balanced environments, etc. Without forests, our lands will be covered by deserts. We will suffer with hunger, hot climate and lack of life materials. Life will be extremely difficult if we have no forests.

Forests have benefited us even more. When we appreciated classical music, let's check how they were created. Then we can see that many of them were products of composers who were very lucky to live in an age when there were exuberant forests everywhere. The peace and beauty of the forests were the indispensable source of the composers' insights. Even now, when we listen to the music, we can also recall the harmony once existing between man and nature.

So let's save the forests. Do not cut down them any more. We should plant and protect them instead. In order to make the world better and life easier for ourselves, our children and our children's children, let's be the gardeners instead of the destroyers. It is the only way.

8. Topic: *Some students like long vacations. Others like several short vacations. Which kind of vacation do you prefer? Give specific reasons for your answer.*

Hello, friends! As students, when are your happiest days?

Holidays! I think everyone will agree with this answer, I know too. But what kind of holiday do you like better, the longer one or several short vacations in a year? I think each of them has its advantages and disadvantages. As for me, I like the latter one.

Now, let's look at the good and bad points of the two kinds of holidays. Of course, I'd like to begin the topic with my favorite one—short vacations. First, short vacations are a great relaxation after busy final exams. When we finish the exams, we know that we will have a month to think freely, to do other things besides classes, to visit friends, to be with our family, to go to concerts, to watch sports contests and so on. Second, we can plan to travel during the short vacation. In spring, we can go to mountains, to see the various flowers that can not be seen in cities, to see the stream flowing, to climb the mountains, and to appreciate the beautiful scenery on the summit! What a wonderful picture, especially for us students who are always swimming in the "sea" of books! And in summer we can go to the seashore to enjoy the sunshine and long beach. In winter we may go to see the snow scenery! It gives us a lot of pleasure. At last, the most important one is that we will not forget classes after the short vacations. The shortcoming is that, for those students who want to make some money to cover their school expenses, the vacations are too short for them to make enough money.

As for the longer vacations, we can have a longer period and relaxation. We can go to remote areas or go abroad to travel. But if we only have one long vacation for a year, isn't it dull for us? And we also may forget some of our lessons after we return to school.

From the above, I think the short period of vacations have a lot more advantages when compared with the longer ones. So why not join us in short holidays and enjoy everything we'd like to do!

9. Topic: *Some universities arrange a long period of vacation for students in the school year, others arrange several short vacations. Which kind of vacation do you prefer—a long vacation or a short one? Give specific reasons and examples for your answer.*

Do you ever go to the Huangshan Mountain in An'hui Province? Do you ever walk along the long corridor of the Summer Palace in Beijing? Do you ever feel the softness of the West Lake in Hangzhou?

I remember the pleasant journey to the Huangshan Mountain I once took. When we, my classmates and I, arrived at the foot of the mountain at about 5 a.m, it was still dark. The mountains looked like black giants standing around us. We began to climb up. Although it was very hot in the summer, we felt very cool there. We climbed and climbed while the sun rose. All the scenes became clear in our eyes. I could see "the Flying Stone" far away. The sky was so blue, and we could hear the birds chirping; all was so quiet. We walked along without a word, enjoying the wonderfulness of the sound of silence. Oh, it was so great and it is beyond my description.

It took me about fifteen days to have a trip to the Huangshan Mountain. If I had not had such a long vacation, I would never have had a chance to make so nice a journey.

I like long vacations, but it is not just because I can have a long period of time to take a long trip during a long vacation, but also I can do many things. I can study the things I am interested in but have no time to study in my routine days; I can find a job to obtain the necessary experiences I need for my career, etc. There are always so many interesting and useful things to do during a long vacation.

In a short vacation, I would have no idea how to plan for it. It is always so short that I can not even complete one thing. The only thing I could do is stay at home, sleeping, eating and making myself fatter and fatter.

I like long vacations. But for all the people, no matter how long or how short the vacation is, the most important thing is to remember that a vacation is a period of time you enjoy yourself, a period of time you do something useful and interesting. If you did do something you are interested in, it would be a nice vacation no matter it is long or short.

10. Topic: ***A research center is going to be established in a university. There is an argument about whether to establish an agricultural research center or a business one. Which do you think is better? Use specific reasons to support your answer.***

Although the Chinese used to think that agriculture was the most fundamental as well as essential aspect of our national economy, with the opening of our door, more and more Chinese people have come to realize the importance of business. We cannot isolate ourselves any longer: we must trade with other nations; we must make our country a truly powerful nation. Therefore, if we are only to set up a business research center or an agricultural research center, we had better choose the former for three specific reasons.

First, we must realize that in modern society, a nation depending on agriculture can never become an advanced country. We can not lag behind in an agricultural era. Some developed countries such as the USA, Japan and Germany have already surpassed this period. They caught the opportunity and developed into industrial age. That is why those nations become so powerful and advanced.

Second, with the opening policy coming into every Chinese mind, we now face a golden opportunity to develop our business theory. Chinese have begun to learn about the functions of market and stock market and so on. These new things attract more and more people. But few of them really understand how to use these new tools, so a business research center has become imperative for us.

Finally, to trade with foreigners and to get advanced techniques from them require us to acquire enough knowledge and skills to level the playing filed. We must know not only our own system, but theirs as well, so we can succeed in negotiating and trading.

An open China has realized the importance of business. Why should we give up this opportunity to rely on agriculture instead? It is the right time for us to make a historical choice.

11. Topic: *Some people like to listen to classical music, others like to listen to popular music (including popular songs) Which kind of music do you prefer? Give specific reasons for your answer.*

Music is the source of wit. Good music can enlighten people's heart. Classical music is more complex and profound than popular music. They are the main components of music. Some people like classics and others like the popular stuff. This is due to the different comprehension of music. There are many young people, including me, who especially like popular music.

There are many kinds of popular music, such as rock music, heavy metal, easy listening and so on. Despite all the differences among them, they have many similar merits.

First, they come from the real lives and they are far more accessible to the youngsters. Most people like something very close to them, because they want to be relaxed. Classical music is a little far away and requires some special knowledge for people to appreciate it. A popular song, like "Let It Be" or "One Hundred Miles", is very simple. When one listens to it, he can easily understand what the singer sings.

Second, most popular music is written about love , a theme most youngsters care much for. Popular music has a very important expression: the association of music and words. When people listen to it, they first listen to the words of it, then the rhythm and other contents. Youngsters have many romantic dreams about love. When a singer sings what they have been trying to say, he will really feel very good. I have a friend who felt very sad when he lost his love. But after several days, I found that he became calm. I asked him why. He told me he had just heard a popular song which encourages people not to be sad because there are many chances ahead of them.

Third, there are strong feelings in the popular music. We youngsters have many strong feelings about the world. We want to express them. Many popular songs have helped us to attain this object. Some music, such as rock music, can easily evoke the resonance among young people. When I fail in something or I succeed in doing something, I want to listen to rock music. After letting my strong feeling out, I become calm and begin to do other things.

In a word, popular music has almost all what we want, especially the same feeling to this world. We like it. At the same time, I can not deny there are also many merits in the classical music.

I can not appreciate it very much because I can not really comprehend it. Perhaps when I am older, I will like it more.

12. Topic: *How do movies or TV influence people's behavior? Use reasons and specific examples to support your answer.*

Just imagine that it is Saturday evening. What will you probably do tonight? I think lots of people will choose to go to movies or stay at home to watch an interesting TV program:

movies have played an important role in our daily life.

First of all, they widen our horizons. There are numerous TV programs concerning worldwide affairs. I can still remember clearly when I first saw the African tribes on the screen. I was fascinated by the marvelous jungles, the colorful weapons, the furious animals and the fantastic wild games. Isn't it marvelous to see the people and places totally different from yours? You would never know them, appreciate them or want to visit them if you have not encountered them on that gigantic screen.

Secondly, they are very entertaining. After a day of hard work, maybe you do not have the energy to go on a long camping trip, especially when you still have lots of things to do tomorrow morning. Why not turn on the TV and choose an interesting show or an exciting game? While having some coffee or chatting with your family, you can really feel relaxed.

Furthermore, as a convenient communication tool, movies, especially TV programs, help the people in the areas of social work, education, advertisements and so on. There is an interesting program called "Let's get to know each other tonight", which helps young men and women to choose their lovers on the screen. Many people like to see it. It becomes so popular that nearly everyone can sing the song in that program.

On the other hand, there are some complaints about TV. For example, some children spend hours before the little screen, ignoring their study, outdoor activities and even their family. Parents say that these kids are indifferent to nearly everything and somehow premature.

As for me, I like to see movies very much. I think every good film is a creative product of mankind. They are useful and instructive as well as entertaining, yet it is true we should tell the kids to spend their time wisely on having other hobbies and other outdoor activities. The same is true for adults. Chocolate is very delicious, but if you eat it everyday, it will be tasteless and maybe disgusting as well as bad to your health.